"Elliott Hughes' *UFOs & Extraterrestrials: Why They Are Here...* is essential, very highly recommended reading for everyone who has been curious about unidentified flying objects from antiquity to the present day. Scholarly, iconoclastic, informative, challenging, illuminating and insightful."

-Midwest Book Review

"*UFOs & Extraterrestrials: Why They Are Here...*is one of the most provocative examinations of humanity's origins I have ever read. It is by far one of the most fascinating works available on the issue of the human race, our extraterrestrial relations, and our immanent future, as we embark on our own odyssey of do- creating new life forms for new purposes."

-Zohara Hieronimus – radio host of "The Zoh Show" and "Future Talk"

"Exciting read; a little shocking. We know they are here. The question is, "Why are they here?" Rather than address the ET issue in the usual way, Roswell, lights in the sky, etc., Hughes takes the reader back to the beginnings of humankind. Following the lead of Sitchin, Von Daniken, and Cayce, with help from the Bible, he shows specifically how and why 'the Adam' was fashioned by the Anunnaki. Unless you are familiar with Cayce, the why will astound you. At first one wants to say, 'impossible,' but Hughes does a good job of presenting evidence that makes the impossible seem possible. Clear and concisely written."

-Pat Alfano, reviewer with Unknown Magazine

ELLIOTT HUGHES

UFOS &

EXTRATERRESTRIALS:
WHY THEY ARE HERE

THE DARKEST, LONGEST KEPT
SECRET IN HUMAN HISTORY

Palmetto Publishing Group
Charleston, SC

UFOs & Extraterrestrials: Why They Are Here
Copyright © 2001 by Elliott Hughes
All rights reserved

First Edition

Printed in the United States

ISBN-13: 978-0-9707873-6-1
ISBN-10: 0-9707873-6-7

"*The most interesting thing about all this material, the most important thing, the haunting thing, is that in the past half-century it has slowly stripped itself of all the illusion, the armies in the sky, the fairies, the incubi, the glorious creatures of old, and come down to what it really is: a difficult experience, terribly enigmatic, the very existence of which implies that we very well maybe something different from what we believe ourselves to be, on this earth for reasons that may not yet be known to us, the understanding of which will be an immense challenge.*"

-Whitley Strieber (*Communion*)

"*We may discover that the ancient world, the further one goes back in time, tends to develop a more and more odd flavor. The mysteries become denser, the strangeness thicker and more viscous.*"

-Robert K.G. Temple (*The Sirius Mystery*)

ACKNOWLEDGEMENTS

No research work of significance is created in a vacuum or is possible without "standing on the shoulders of the giants" who have gone before. No research work of significance is possible without studying the efforts of those who blazed trails of ingenuity, insight, and daring. *UFOs & Extraterrestrials: Why They Are Here—the Darkest, Longest Kept Secret in Human History (Revised Edition)* would not have been possible without the status quo defying research and books by such authors as Erich Von Daniken, Samuel Noah Kramer, Zecharia Sitchin, Edgar Cayce, Robert K.G. Temple, Ruth Montgomery, and Merlin Stone. All wrote books that explored alternative venues of investigation. We give a heartfelt thanks to their dedication and effort and to their unwavering pursuit of what they saw.

We would also like to thank Dr. Jared Diamond for making the latest findings of anthropology understandable to the average curious reader. And Clarissa, who took time to proofread and edit the book.

CONTENTS

INTRODUCTION

FORGET ROSWELL

"And Moses brought forth the people out of the camp to meet with God; and they stood at the nether part of the mount. And mount Sinai was altogether on smoke, because the Lord descended upon it in fire: and the smoke there of ascended as the smoke of a furnace, and the whole mount quaked greatly."

Exodus 19:17-18

For the last several decades, a tremendous debate has been raging. The focus of the debate has been whether or not a UFO actually crashed on a farm, near Roswell Air Force base, in New Mexico, in July1947.

Anyone who is even mildly interested in the UFO phenomena has heard the story of the Roswell crash. The story is true UFO folklore and has survived for 50 years primarily because of several headlines that appeared the following day in the local Roswell daily newspaper, *The Daily Record*. According to documentation, *The Daily Record* had been tipped off to the story by the Air Force commanding officers or their press agents. The headlines dated Tuesday, July 8th, 1947, read, *"USAAF Captures Flying Saucer On Ranch in Roswell Region."* The sub headlines read, *"No Details of Flying Disk Are Revealed,"* and, *"Hardware Man and Wife Report Disk Seen."*

UFO proponents site these headlines and that the lead for the stories came from the Air Force commanding officers as proof that something strange happened. The very next day, however, the Air Force brass recanted the original story and claimed that it had all been an embarrassing mistake. It had really been a "weather balloon" that had been recovered." Sorry, folks."

What actually happened that rainy, stormy evening on July7, in 1947, has been the focus of heated arguments and debates ever since. Professional and amateur UFO researchers and pragmatic UFO skeptics, attempting to either prove or disprove the reality of the UFO phenomena, have focused on the Roswell alleged UFO crash as ammunition for their arguments.

At least two high ranking Pentagon officials have come forward with books about what has been an alleged government cover-up that has spanned the past fifty years: *Majestic*, a book written by Whitley Strieber, claims to be the fictionalized though actual memoirs of Roscoe Hillenkoetter, the then (1947) Director of the CIA. Mr. Strieber claims he was given boxes full of Roswell documents by the dying Hillenkoetter. Interestingly, the book claims that Roscoe Hillenkoetter had been abducted by extraterrestrials many times, beginning when he was a small child.

Perhaps the most startling revelation to come out of the book *Majestic* was the conclusion Mr. Strieber arrives at whereby not only does he present documentation that the Roswell UFO crash actually happened, but that it had been no accident.

That Roswell had been a deliberate attempt by the extraterrestrials to take humans to the next level of awareness of their existence.

In The *Day After Roswell*, by Col. Philip J. Corso (Ret.), where Col. Corso reveals that it had been his job, as head of the Foreign Technologies Division of the Army, to keep the technologies found at the Roswell UFO crash site classified; to find practical applications for the new technologies; and filter them into American industries by quietly making the new technologies available to the army defense contractors. Col. Corso claims that "laser, fiber optics, printed circuit technology, night-vision or infrared technologies, the Kevlar material in bulletproof vest, and accelerated particle-beam devices," just to name a few, all came from "back-engineering" the *debris* found at the Roswell crash site.

The Roswell *Daily Record's* headlines and newspaper articles appearing the day after the alleged UFO crash, and the revelations contained in the books *Majestic*, and *The Day After Roswell* are strong indications that there exist hard physical evidence of both UFOs and extraterrestrials. But because of the government and military's persistent position of denial on the Roswell UFO crash, many very intelligent, very pragmatic people do not believe UFOs or extraterrestrials exist. Their skepticism is understandable. There is, however, another way to investigate the reality or the illusion of the UFO phenomena.

If you are really interested in the scientific validation (proof) of the UFO phenomena, you've got to realize two things: First, the government and the military will never admit there has been a cover-up. It is not in their best interest to do so. At first, the cover-up was viewed as a wartime necessity. The intentions of the beings that piloted the crashed UFO were not known. Perhaps the crashed vessel was an advanced scout ship probing our defenses. Our Air Force officials did not believe it was a coincidence that the UFO crashed near White Sands, a very sensitive military installation (in the Roswell, New Mexico desert) where the bombers that carried our hydrogen bombs-- the ones that leveled Hiroshima-were stationed. July 1947 was only about two years after that nuclear display of destruction. Maybe there was a connection. Maybe not. They didn't know. Our military officials took what they thought was the prudent course of action. They wanted to keep the American people from panicking.

In *The Day After Roswell*, Col. Corso mentions how, in 1938, the Orson Welles radio hoax, that Earth was being invaded by hostile Martians, had really shaken up the American public. The panic over the Orson Welles' radio hoax was still fresh in the minds of the American people and our military. These are responsible people, and careers were at stake. How would the American public have reacted to the reality of actual unknown flying vessels, able to invade our air space at will, able to fly rings around anything we had then or now in our Air Force arsenal of jets or strategic weapons, with unknown weapons capabilities? How would the American public have reacted to the knowledge that these unknown, possibly, hostile aliens have been known to abduct American citizens at will, and that their government is powerless to stop these abductions?

Looking at the big picture, our military did the only logical thing it could do. Denied it. Classified it. And studied it until they could come up with some feasible answers and possibly a plan of action.

Understand that what began as necessity to quell public panic and in the interest of National Security took on its own momentum or inertia. Our government and military won't tell now because the institutions of denial have become too deeply entrenched, too much a part of tradition, and it is still the safest, most politically astute position to take. Too many high-profile officials and politicians may be embarrassed. Too many explanations would be necessary. It is easier to maintain the accepted status quo and the traditional stance of denial.

So, don't hold your breath waiting for the Pentagon or government to tell you, "Yeah, we covered-up the Roswell thing. We did it for your own good. We're sorry, but it had to be done." It won't happen. That's not the way things work.

Second, FORGET Roswell: If you're really interested in discovering the proof of the reality of UFOs and extraterrestrials, and why they are here, forget Roswell. Pretend it never happened. Forget the last fifty years and the rumors of an alien invasion. That is not what the UFO phenomena is about. Forget the thousands of UFO sightings reported by no-nonsense police officers, airline and military pilots, commercial and military radar technicians clocking unidentified bogies on their radar screens; forget the reports of UFO sightings by United States astronauts or naval submarine crews; forget the thousands of alleged UFO photographs, some fakes, some unexplainable; forget the Whitley Striebers and the Bud Hopkins and their tales of alien abductions; forget "Dreamland" (Area 51), Roswell, and "back-engineered" technologies; forget "God's" landing on Mount Sinai, in a "roar and a pillar of fire and smoke;" forget Ezekiel's reported flight in a "flying chariot;" forget Neanderthal cave drawings of UFOs that date back tens of thousands of years. Don't get the wrong idea. These are all forms of empirical evidence in their own right. But the skeptics have had a long time to contemplate scenarios that explain these proofs away.

The problem with Roswell and these other proofs are that they are too narrow a focus. Fifty years is an insufficient focus to explain the reported UFO and extraterrestrial activities that have spanned millenniums. The proof that has not yet been tampered with, or that has not yet been explained away, lies approximately 100,000 years in antiquity and beyond, in the long-forgotten beginning, in anthropology and the theories of the origins of Man. Where humankind begins, where the anomaly of kinks in the evolutionary flow in the timeline of a species of large primates called apes, where these Darwinian evolutionary anomalies baffle and defy explanations by our best scientific minds, *that's* where to seek the proof of the existence of UFOs and extraterrestrials. That's where the mystery of *why* they are here begins to make sense.

UFOs, extraterrestrials, and the origin of the human species- that's where it all began. That's where the dark secret lies, and the irrefutable proof of their existence. In antiquity, in the dark dream-like beginning, and in the somber answer to a single innocent question: How did we get here?

In *UFOs &Extraterrestrials: Why They Are Here-The Darkest, Longest Kept Secret in Human History* (Revised Edition), we will scientifically investigate and prove the existence of UFOs and extraterrestrials, partially, using orthodox scientific fields of study, and logical pragmatic analysis of known existing data. Much of this data appears in the Judeo-Christian Bible. Please understand that this UFO study is NOT an attack on religion, nor should it be considered a religious treatise. It is an attempt to scientifically arrive at the truth, by whatever means necessary and available.

There is some conjecture, and gaps in understanding where we cannot even hazard a guess. But for the most part, the picture that emerges from the UFO puzzle pieces together fits the known scientific and religious understanding of the evolution of our species, and, therefore, will prove that extraterrestrials not only had a hand in the creation of *Homo sapiens*, but that they have been an omnipresent influence in our evolution ever since.

Love long, and prosper.

-Elliott M Hughes

Nov. 2004

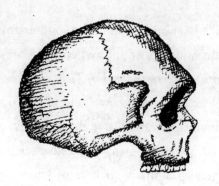

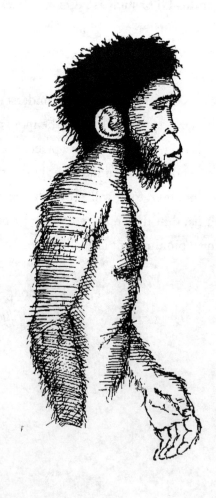

CHAPTER 1:

THE SCIENTIFIC VALIDATION OF UFOS & EXTRATERRESTRIALS, OR PROBLEMS WITH THE TIMELINE

> *"The identity of the ingredient that produced the Great Leap Forward poses an archaeological puzzle without an accepted answer. "*
>
> -Jared Diamond
>
> (*The Third Chimpanzee*, 1992)

f UFOs and extraterrestrials exist, where is the empirical evidence that undisputedly proves the reality of their existence? Stated another way, are there any fields of study in accepted realms of modern science that either hint at, or flat out point to the conclusion that Earth has visited by intelligent life forms from other planets or other dimensions at any time in humankind's present or past?

There is.

Empirical evidence does exist. The accepted realms of modern science that provide this evidence are paleontology (the study of fossils), archaeology, anthropology, and molecular biology, as it relates to DNA backdating of bone fragments. Contributing to the hard, physical evidence is a common denominator factor that underlies the etiology (the origins) of all the major religions of the human species. The proof of the existence of UFOs and extraterrestrials lies in the scientific investigation of the origin of the human species. *The scientific investigation of how we got here is where the untampered, uncensored evidence lies.*

To seek proof from the alleged UFO related events of the past fifty years is too narrow a focus. And it's not that there haven't been any significant UFO events in the past fifty years. There have been. It's just that our present materialistic scientific worldview insists on a kind of, "if you can't cut it, weigh it, or measure it," it has no reality in our present scientific paradigm. Since the government and military agencies that maybe in possession of the hard, physical evidence are denying any evidence exist, we are left with mostly speculation, photographs, our own experiences and research, and whatever we can find on the Internet in the way of proof.

Our solution is to circumvent these roadblocks and official denials by realizing that the evidence of the existence of extraterrestrials is not solely in the possession of government and military agencies. Our solution is to realize that evidence of extraterrestrial contact did not begin a mere fifty years ago, or one hundred years ago, or even several millenniums ago. No. In fact, our proof of the existence of UFOs and extraterrestrials begins with the scientific *and* religious understanding of how we got here. That's right. It's not an either/or proposition because both scientific and religious disciplines hold valuable clues. In fact, only by synthesizing all of the fragments of information we have from science, religion, and metaphysics can we arrive at a total understanding of the origin of the human species, its connectedness to extraterrestrials, and the proof and understanding of why they are here.

Science and the Origin of the Human Species

Ironically, one of the most enduring mysteries of modern science is the enigma of exactly where the human species came from. Religious schools of thought say that we are all descendants of Adam and Eve, who the Lord God created in the Garden of Eden. Scientists don't put much stock in this creationism theory partially because of the difficulty in proving the existence of God (though DNA research has proven the reality of both Adam and Eve).[1]

Another reason scientists don't put much stock in creationism is because they believe they already know the broad details of how we got here. The entire picture is not completely clear, but most of it is there: From carbon dating and DNA analysis of the fossilized remains of bone fragments, skulls, and artifacts, scientists believe that the human species evolved from apes. All of the physical evidence gathered from paleontology, archaeology and anthropology support this Darwinian theory of the origin and evolution of the human species.

Cousins

We are obviously related to apes: We're both mammals. We're both primates. We both tend to walk upright. Have hair. Nurse our young. Have flat finger and toe nails instead of claws. Thumbs. "A penis that hangs freely rather than being attached to the abdomen." We resemble each other, i.e., we look alike.

So sure, in fact, were scientists that humans evolved from the lower primates that the only thing they weren't completely sure about was *which* of the lower primates was our "closest" relative. Are we genetically closer to monkeys (monkeys have tails, apes don't), or one of the species of apes; gibbons, orangutans, gorillas, or chimpanzees?

The debate continued until the 1980's, when scientists (Charles Sibley and Jon Ahlquist) began using a process that had been successful in classifying thousands of different species of birds, to answer this "closest" relative question. This process was a method of using the DNA molecule (the DNA molecule is present in all animal and in all plant cells and determines size, shape, coloring, habits, etc.) to calibrate how much time has passed since similar species shared a common ancestor.

DNA Backdating

If similar species were derived from a common ancestor (say humans, apes, and monkeys), they, at one time, had identical forms of the DNA molecule. That is, at some point in pre-history, humans, apes and monkeys must have been essentially the same creature, same size, same shape, same coloring, same sexual habits, same DNA.

Then, for some unknown, mysterious reason, which we can only guess was caused by evolution, the molecules that determine size, shape, coloring, and habits, etc.[the DNA molecule], among *some* of the members of this common ancestor species, mutated.

Assuming that the rate of change (the rate of genetic mutation) is uniform, and that we know how many changes occurred in, say, a million year period, the present differences between the DNA molecules of humans and the DNA molecules of monkeys and apes could be used as a "clock" to calibrate how many millions of years have passed since humans, monkeys, and apes shared a common ancestor. The species whose DNA most resembles human DNA, or that shows the least percentage of difference from human DNA, would be our "closest" relative in the animal kingdom.

DNA Hybridization

How do we determine what the genetic difference is between monkeys, apes and humans? "A quick method of measuring changes in DNA structure is to mix the DNA from two species, then measure by how many degrees of temperature the melting point of the mixed (hybrid) DNA is reduced below the melting point of pure DNA from a single species. The method is generally referred to as "DNA hybridization.' As it turns out, a melting point lowered by one degree centigrade means that the DNAs of the two species differ by roughly 1 percent.[3] Using this method, it turns out that human DNA differs from monkey DNA by 7%. Not all that great of a "genetic distance," but it still indicates that we are genetically closer to apes than monkeys.

Our "genetic distance" from gibbons shortens to 5%. Our "genetic distance" from orangutans is only 3.6%. Human DNA gets even closer to a match with gorilla DNA exhibiting only a 2.3% difference. But, as it turns out, "the chimpanzee, not the gorillas are our closest relative. Put another way, the chimpanzee's closest relative is not the gorilla but humans.[4]"

Our "genetic distance" from both the common chimpanzee and the pygmy chimpanzee is a startling 1.6%.

In fact, human DNA is so similar to chimpanzee DNA that, zoologically speaking, "humans are technically not a separate family at all but should be considered a third species of chimpanzees.[5]"

So, based on observable, fossil, commonsense and DNA evidence, just as Charles Darwin postulated in 1859, our evolution from apes seems to be a foregone, scientific conclusion. Case closed.

The Darwinian theory that humans evolved from apes could almost be considered scientific fact, if not for a couple of major glitches. Glitch # 1 happened about 100,000 years ago. Glitch #2 happened from 40,000 to 28,000 years ago. These "glitches" are called the "missing links."

How does the Darwinian theory of evolution explain the "missing links"? To date, it cannot.

The "Missing Links"

For DNA backdating and DNA hybridization to be more than scientific flights of fancy, the assumption that genetic mutations occur at a uniform rate should be valid. If genetic mutations do not occur at a uniform rate, then all of the dates established by these methods are worthless.

There are at least two major instances, in the evolution of the human species, where the rate of genetic mutation is not uniform. These evolutionary anomalies have been referred to as "the missing links," but what they really refer to are discrepancies in the evolutionary timeline. These discrepancies are what we would like you to pay close attention to.

From bone fragments, skulls, partial or complete skeletons, DNA and carbon dating of stone tools and artifacts, anthropologists believe that humanity's evolution from the lower primates proceeded something like this:

I.   **Several billion years ago:** Life originated on Earth.

II. **65 million years ago:** Dinosaurs became extinct.

III. **Between 6 and 10 million years ago:** The species of apes split into apes and a species of upright hominids (man-apes more animal than man).

IV. **4 million years ago:** The structure of fossilized limb bones shows that our ancestors were habitually walking upright on two hind limbs.

V.   **3 million years ago:** Our lineage split again producing:
     a. *Australopithecus Robustus* ("the robust southern ape")
     b. *Australopithecus Africanus* ("the southern ape of Africa") *Australopithecus Africanus* evolved into *Homo habilis* ("man the handyman").

VI. **1,700,000 years ago:** The differences were so great anthropologists gave a new name to our lineage—*Homo erectus.*

7

VII. **1,000,000 years ago:** *Homo erectus* began to migrate. Peking man and Java man resided in Asia.

VIII. **500,000 years ago:** *Homo erectus* could be classified as *Homo sapiens* -pre- Neanderthal *Homo sapiens.*

IX. **130,000 to 74,000 years ago:** There were three species of man-apes:

    a. a) Neanderthals lived in western Europe, southern Russia, Central Asia near Afghanistan.

    b. *Australopithecus Africanus* ("the southern ape of Africa") suddenly has mysteriously modern anatomy (100,000 years ago).

    c. In eastern Asia, people unlike either the Neanderthals or Africans.

X. **50,000 to 40,000 years ago:** there were 3 species of man-apes.

    a. In Europe and western Asia lived Neanderthals.

    b. In Africa, people increasingly like us moderns in their anatomy.

    c. In eastern Asia, people unlike either the Neanderthals or Africans.

XI. **40,000 years ago:** Cro-Magnons were fully anatomically modern (they physically looked like us) 40,000 years ago! Their anatomy, 40,000 years ago, was so much akin to ours that Dr. Diamond makes the statement, "Had one of these gentlemen or ladies strolled down Champs Elysees [Street] in modern attire, he or she would not. have stood out from the Parisian crowd in any way."

Cro-Magnons had: 1) bone needles for sewing; 2) stone axes with wooden handles, whose heads were made from stone slithers that were 10 times sharper than Neanderthal's stone tools; 3) flutes, rattles; 4) necklaces, art 5) lamps.

This is essentially the timeline that modern anthropologists believe traces humankind's origins. The "kinks" in this evolutionary timeline are also the reason a purely Darwinian theory of evolution of the human species makes no sense, at least, not at the period of the emergence of the modern (anatomically speaking) Africans 100,000 years ago. Darwinian evolution falls apart again at the period of 40,000 years ago, with the too early appearance of Cro-Magnons.

The appearance of Cro-Magnons was the other problem both in terms of their sudden intelligence (innovation) and their sudden actual appearance. Scientists initially believed that Neanderthals had evolved into Cro-Magnons. That was the accepted theory on how Cro-Magnons got here.

That theory was discarded, however, when the skeletons of still anatomically primitive Neanderthals were found dating back to just after 40,000 years ago. The problem was that skeletons of fully anatomically modern Cro-Magnons had been found in Europe, dating back to the same period (40,000). If anatomically modern Cro-Magnons were found in Europe dating back to 40,000 years ago, and still anatomically primitive Neanderthals were found dating back to the same period, then, Cro-Magnons did not evolve from Neanderthals. When

Cro-Magnons appeared, there should no longer have been any trace of primitive Neanderthals dating back to the same period. Because of these more recent findings, the more current scientific conclusion is that Cro-Magnons did *not* evolve from Neanderthals.

This discovery created a new mystery: If Cro-Magnons did not evolve from Neanderthals, where did they come from?

Dr. Diamond does not address this mystery. He does address the mystery of the sudden appearance of innovation among a formerly intellectually dull species:

"Thus, we have a tentative picture of anatomically modern people arising in Africa over a hundred thousand years ago, but initially making the same tools as Neanderthals...By perhaps sixty thousand years ago, some **magic twist** of behavior had been added to the modern anatomy. The twist produced innovative, fully modern people." [p.53]

-Dr. Jared Diamond
The Third Chimpanzee, 1992

The closest Dr. Diamond comes to explaining this sudden evolutionary advancement in *Homo sapiens*' innovative skills and intelligence is to call it "some magic twist of behavior," i.e., modern science, anthropologists don't have a clue as to what this "magic twist of behavior" was. The theory postulated by Dr. Diamond and other anthropologists is that whatever the magic twist was it produced the ability to talk and communicate in language. The source of the twist is not even guessed at. Apparently, it just happened.

In *The Third Chimpanzee*, this mysterious period in human evolution is underscored by Dr. Diamond's naming Chapter Two "The Great Leap Forward" and stating openly that "the identity of the ingredient that produced the Great Leap Forward poses an archaeological puzzle without an accepted answer." The inexplicable appearance of fully anatomically modern *Australopithecus Africanus* ("the southern African ape") 100,000 years ago and the sudden appearance of Cro-Magnons and their so much greater intelligence than the simultaneously living Neanderthals 40,000 years ago are the holes (the "missing links") in accepting a purely Darwinian theory of human evolution. For one, it happened much too quickly. For another, it made no sense. If Neanderthals did not evolve into Cro-Magnons, where did Cro-Magnons come from? And why were there no sites found in Africa or Europe or any where else of Cro-Magnons prior to 40,000 years ago? Shouldn't there have been some traces of their growing innovation?[6]

The main problem was that it happened too soon much, much, too soon to be the result of pure evolution. A puzzle piece is missing.

"For most of the six million years since our lineage diverged from that of apes, we remained little more than glorified chimpanzees in how we made our living. As recently as forty thousand years ago, western Europe was still occupied by Neanderthals, primitive beings for whom art and progress scarcely existed. Then came an abrupt change, as anatomically modern people appeared in Europe bringing with them art, musical instruments, lamps, trade, and progress. Within a short time Neanderthals were gone."

-Jared Diamond
The Third Chimpanzee

CHAPTER 2:

THE "SIGNATURE" OF THE "GODS"

If Cro-Magnons did not evolve from Neanderthals, as scientists originally believed, where did they come from? This question is still largely unanswered by mainstream science. As far as conventional anthropologists are concerned, Cro-Magnons' sudden appearance, sudden innovative skills and sudden culture, 40,000 years ago, remains an enigma--a mystery wrapped in a riddle, as unfathomable and incomprehensible as time travel.

Yet, because the fossil evidence of Cro-Magnons exists, "something" obviously happened. "Something" produced a species of anatomically modern though still intellectually primitive *Homo sapiens* 100,000 years ago (anatomically modem Africans), while Neanderthals of the same period, still looked like thickskulled, sloped fore headed, knuckle-walking, smelly, grunting cavemen. Tool making-wise, innovation-wise, intelligence and art-wise, the moderns and the Neanderthals were both stuck in the same evolutionary level of dull intelligence for about 60,000 years, a virtual eternity. Then, unexplainably, suddenly, "something" produced in Cro-Magnons the "magical twist of behavior" that allowed Cro-Magnons to evolve into the dominate species of man-apes, and to ultimately survive, while the species of Neanderthals became extinct.

Looking at this enigma from a realistic, pragmatic, scientific perspective, what are the possible explanations for this "Great Leap Forward?" What really happened 100,000 years ago that initially produced "anatomically modern" *Australopithecus Africanus*, then again 40,000 years ago produced the intelligent, cultured Cro-Magnons? What was Cro-Magnons' (and therefore all of humanity's) true origin, if the etiology of our existence was not one of purely evolutionary means?--HOW DID WE GET HERE!? And what does the anomaly of Cro-Magnons' sudden appearance have to do with our attempt to prove the flesh and blood reality of UFOs and extraterrestrials?

The Myth of the Primitive "Myth"

The solution to the mystery of Cro-Magnons' sudden appearance and sudden intelligence, as well as the empirical evidence of the reality of UFOs and extraterrestrials, was discovered in an archaeological dig some 180 years ago. At the time, however, no one realized that the unearthed ancient texts and artifacts were the solution to the timeline anomaly, or that the ancient texts proved the reality of extraterrestrials. No one made the connection because although the discovery was seen as a fascinating anthropological find, it was seen as merely the texts of the culture, superstitions, and "myths" of a primitive and scientifically naïve people.

14

Sumer: Another Anomaly

The ancient civilization that was discovered was Sumer. Sumer is the oldest, most highly advanced civilization so far unearthed by archaeologists. It is estimated that the Sumerian civilization pre-dates both ancient Egypt (3100 B.C.) and Babylon (2500 B.C.) by several thousand years. Scholars believe Sumer flourished between 5,500 and 8,000 years ago (3,500 to 6,000 B.C.).

Sumer is another piece of empirical evidence of the reality of extraterrestrials. It, like the modem anatomy of *Australopithecus Africanus* ("the southern ape of Africa"), and the intelligence and culture of Cro-Magnons, is a bit of a mystery to scholars.

In *The 12th Planet*, Zecharia Sitchin called it "The Sudden Civilization." It was a surprisingly highly technologically and culturally advanced civilization that seemed to appear full blown out of nowhere. Its achievements, even today, boggles the imagination. The more that is understood about Sumer, the more truly amazing it seems.

For example, one of the things archaeologists and anthropologists did not expect to find in an 8,000-year-old civilization were libraries! There were libraries full of completely intact books (clay tablets). There were books on medicine, surgery, mathematics, farming, methods of payment of debts, civil laws, courts, schoolbooks, taxes, cooking recipes and poems. The first bricks fortified with chopped straw were made in Sumer; the first Farmer's Almanac; the first calendar; the first system of mathematics; the first system of mathematics based on base 60; the 360 degrees in a circle is a remnant of ancient Sumerian mathematics or geometry, as is the 12 inches in a foot.[1] The wheel!

The first furnace that "could produce intense but controlled heat that would not contaminate products with dust or ashes" was invented in Sumer. This furnace was called a *kiln*, and "made possible an even greater technological advance: the Age of Metals."[2]

To produce the intense heat necessary to smelt ores and create metals, fuels were necessary. "The fuels that made Sumer technologically supreme were bitumens[3] and asphalts, petroleum products that naturally seeped up to the surface in many places in Mesopotamia."[4]

So, among their already numerous remarkable achievements, add that the Sumerians discovered petroleum products as fuels and were the inventors of the Iron and the Bronze Ages.

Sumer came from seemingly out of nowhere and achieved one of the most highly advanced civilization *Homo sapiens* have ever known. The real questions here are, how do an ancient and primitive people come by a virtual prefabricated civilization? How is that possible? How did they create an alphabet, for instance? How did they learn how to write? How did they come by an understanding of the workings of the human body so in depth that they had surgeons who could remove cataracts from the eye 8,000 years ago? By comparison, in more recent times, Leonardo De Vinci [1452 – 1519], had to dissect the bodies of cadavers for his study of the human body's internal organs. His drawings of human anatomy were considered great advances in understanding in the 1500s. How did the ancient

Sumerians know more about human anatomy than Leonardo De Vinci?

Where did the Sumerians get the idea to make a furnace that could produce intense, controlled heat that would not contaminate what was being heated with ash or dust? Where did an ancient people, who had been using stone tools for about 400,000 years (or probably longer), suddenly get an idea to make something you don't even know exists?

Or, where did the Sumerians get the idea to use petroleum products to fuel those new furnaces? Do you see the problem here? Maybe one or two of these advances would have been possible for an ancient, innovative people. By luck or by accident a few of these innovations could have come into being. But taken as a whole, the entire Sumerian civilization, there was far too much technology far too soon to have been all thought up by a handful of Neo-Stone Age *Homo sapiens*, 8,000 years ago, or even 5,000 years ago.

Our empirical evidence here is not simply that this level of technological advancement and culture should have been unheard of 8,000 years ago. It is two things: first, it has the same M.O. (method of operation) as the Cro-Magnon mystery--*Homo sapiens* suddenly, inexplicably demonstrating a vast unprecedented level of understanding, intelligence or culture seemingly overnight; the second part of this empirical evidence scientifically validating the flesh and blood reality of extraterrestrials is what the Sumerians themselves had to say about their culture and technological advances. According to their own records, the Sumerians did not achieve their technological advances and high culture alone. They say they had help.

Of course, the ancient Sumerians did not call their helpers "extraterrestrials." The word would have had no meaning to them. They called their tutors, their instructors, their teachers, "gods." They claim that the "gods" instructed them. Told them what to do, and how to do it. They say their help came from the "gods," or the "messengers of the gods," also called "angels of the gods."

That the Sumerians had reached such an unprecedented high level of technological advances and culture, and that *they* attributed those advances to the "gods," is empirical evidence in that the technological advances are still observable —not theoretical—and it is highly unlikely that an ancient culture could have achieved so much unaided.

That the Sumerians had help is almost self-evident. That they readily admit that they had help should be believed. Again, it is the Cro-Magnon puzzle on a much grander scale: sudden appearance, sudden innovative skills and intelligence, sudden cultural and high technological advances--"sudden civilization." And like the Cro-Magnon puzzle there are no acceptable, plausible explanations within mainstream science. Yet, it is obvious that if a pattern repeats itself, that is a very strong indication that the same forces or beings were involved.

We submit that the repetition of this pattern of *Homo sapiens* suddenly acquiring new, unheard of levels of innovative and cognitive skills, social graces, and high levels of culture and technology is empirical evidence of the reality of extraterrestrials, provided by mainstream scientists themselves. Science's very model of what happened, how we got here, and what the first highly advanced civilization was like all point to the reality of extraterrestrial intervention in human evolution. It is the only answer that fits all of the variables of how, when, where, and why this intervention could have taken place. This answer alone explains the sudden appearance, the sudden innovative skills, and the sudden cultures.

Our empirical evidence does not stop there. It, in fact, only begins there.

In the ancient libraries, there were texts concerning the origin of humans. These creation texts, however, seemed bizarre, naive and childishly primitive to the scholars who initially translated them from their cuneiform, pictographic original form. They did not make sense to the scholars who discovered them. Consequently, the ancient records concerning the Sumerians' understanding of how humans got here were labeled "creation myths." They were categorized, tagged, and never given a second thought as far as any serious relevancy to humankind's true origins were concerned.

Creation Myths: Why They Were Not Believed

It is not difficult to imagine what happened when these records were first unearthed by archaeologists 180 years ago. The accounts in the ancient texts were too fantastic, too bizarre for scientists 180years ago to believe. The problem was that scientists of 180 years ago had no reference points with which to ascertain the scientific plausibility of the ancient texts: 180 years ago, space travel was unheard of, even in the world's literature. Science fiction literature did not yet exist. "If we, a somewhat evolved society in the 1820's (180 years ago), could not journey among the stars, how could a civilization 5,500· to 8,000 years more primitive than we were journey among the stars?" was the thinking. Scientists then, as now, were guilty of judging what is scientifically possible by what is scientifically possible for us. "If we can't do it, it can't be done" is the traditional scientific paradigm.

The Twilight Zone

To take the archaeologists and anthropologists even further into the Twilight Zone, besides the mention of the "gods" arriving by spaceship, there was also mention of genetic engineering. Of course, the words "genetic engineering" were not used in the ancient texts, but the process could be none other. The ancient texts used the term *"fashioned."* The gods *"fashioned"* the Adama.[5] 180 years ago the idea of genetically engineering ("fashioning") a species of beings would have been deemed scientifically impossible. It would not have been believed. It was not until 1866 that Austrian botanist and monk Gregor Johan Mendel proposed the basic laws of heredity, based on cross breeding experiments with peas.

So the idea of genetically engineering an entire species of beings called humans was equally incomprehensible to the best scientific minds we had in the 1820's.

Since there were no reference points then that spoke of the scientific plausibility of space travel, or the scientific plausibility of genetic engineering, since no source of knowledge then in existence could validate the truth of the ancient Sumerian texts, the only sane conclusion scientists 180 years ago could arrive at was that the texts had to be myths--"creation myths." What else could they be?

Since this was the official, scientific explanation of just what those ancient records were all about, this explanation has stuck and has never been seriously challenged. That is, not until Zecharia Sitchin published his anthropological breakthrough in an eight-book series called *The Earth Chronicles* (1976). *The Earth Chronicles* are linguistic anthropologist Zecharia Sitchin's translations, analysis, and commentary on the ancient Sumerian, Akkadian, and other related texts from antiquity. In *The Earth Chronicles*, Mr. Sitchin boldly proclaims that the ancient texts were ancient "records," not myths, and proceeded to scientifically prove his assertions using linguistics (the original meaning of ancient words), artifacts, ancient maps, trade routes, historical and biblical records and comparisons.

The Earth Chronicles is must reading for any serious researcher of the UFO phenomena. If you are looking for quantity and quality of empirical evidence of the reality of UFOs and extraterrestrials (besides what you will discover here), Zecharia is overkill. He will leave you dazed and reeling from information overload. The sheer quantity of his proof is what will convince even the most pragmatic and skeptical UFO opponent.

All eight books are fascinating, but his revelation closest to our research focus here is the translation of the texts on how and why the ancient people believed humans were created by the "gods." The translation gains in relevancy and interest when we discover that both Sumerologist Samuel Noah Kramer and Zecharia Sitchin say that Genesis is an abridged version of this older Sumerian "creation myth" called the *Enuma elish*. That the Sumerian text is the original that Genesis "borrows" from, indeed, piques our interest. What does this original text, that Genesis is an abridged version of, say is the origin of humans? What does it have to say about the "gods" who created humankind?

These are intriguing questions, but what is equally fascinating is a glaring inconsistency which has to do with the very nature of the Anunnaki, the extraterrestrial beings that, according to the ancient texts, genetically engineered the Adam, humankind. The real mystery, the deeper mystery, is the contradiction of who and what these extraterrestrials portray themselves as. If a God exist, we have been conditioned to expect a loving, caring, powerful, omniscient, sometimes wrathful, but basically benevolent spiritual authority that can tune into our lives as easily as we can tune into Star Trek. God, in His wisdom and power hears or does not hear our prayers, depending on whether or not He thinks we are deserving. We may think of God as good but wrathful.

This is not what we find. By their own admission, they are a warlike, power-hungry, sexually promiscuous and incestuous, highly technologically advanced, though somewhat morally decadent species of three dimensionally focused humanoid beings. They have sex with their own mothers, sisters, daughters, and granddaughters. They marry their sisters. They fight each other to the death in wars where they used humans as pawns. Given who and what they portray themselves as, in the ancient Sumerian texts, why would a species of warlike beings, with highly advanced technology, who were by their own account corrupt, petty, morally decadent, and obviously selfish, why would such creatures bother to create anything that did not directly serve their petty needs? That is what does not make sense. Why would they create humankind? To what end? The reason these beings give, which does seem to fit their self-serving needs, only partially makes sense. The rest is an obvious lie.

Why would these highly technologically advanced, warlike beings, that could have destroyed the entire species of *Homo sapiens* in a whim, or the entire planet if need be, feel a need to lie to creatures they themselves created (i.e., "fashioned"). Was it fear, or some other much darker, much more complex reason?

And for the record, exactly what did the *Enuma elish* (the ancient Sumerian texts) say about how "The Adama" was "fashioned?" How do these ancient records solve the anomaly of the timeline discrepancies? And much more to our point, what were the "gods" lying about, and why? What would a "god" be afraid of? What knowledge was forbidden?

CHAPTER 3

THE *"LULU"*--THE "PRIMITIVE WORKER": THE ORIGIN OF THE HUMAN SPECIES ACCORDING· TO THE *ENUMA ELISH*

> *"Both inform and content, the Biblical books bear no little [i.e., bear a GREAT] resemblance to the literatures created by earlier civilizations in the Near East."*
>
> -Samual Noah Kramer
>
> (From *the Tablets of Sumer* - 1956)

Before It Was Genesis

Both Samuel Kramer and Zecharia Sitchin claim that their translations of the ancient Sumerian texts revealed that the Sumerian texts were the older, *original* versions of many of the books found in the Bible. According to their translation and analysis, Genesis is an "abridged" version of the *Enuma elish*—*the* original Sumerian creation myth. The creation myth you are about to read is a synopsis of the longer, original version of several of the books in Genesis, relative to the creation of Adam.

We couldn't help wondering that if what we now have in the books of Genesis is an "abridged" version, what was edited out, and why? Why was it felt necessary to edit the original texts? Won't this dramatically change meanings? What views about "God" (or the "gods" –the extraterrestrials), woman,

man, and why humans were created have been altered by this "editing" of Genesis?

We will go into greater detail of what was edited out and the resulting psychological, sociological, and religious consequences of this editing in the last chapter, "The Genesis Conspiracy." For now, suffice it to say that what was edited out of Genesis were the events involving the "gods" that led up to the reason the "gods" fashioned "The Adam," i.e., created Adam and Eve in the Garden of Eden. This longer, more detailed Sumerian version is the story behind the story.

In this version, "God" does not simply one day decide to create mankind, as a sort of whim or crowning touch to His creation. In this older, original version of Genesis, an alien female scientist named Ninhursag begins the initial trial and error groundwork genetic experiments that lead to the creation of "The Adam." Her efforts are joined later by her scientist husband Enki. Together they create "The Adam." In the original version of Genesis, "The Adam" is needed and "fashioned" to perform a particular function. It is implied that if there is no need for this function, there is no reason to "fashion" humans. Humans were created to perform a particular function for the "gods."

An Interplanetary Mining Expedition

According to the ancient texts, the Anunnaki are a species of three dimensionally focused, oxygen breathing, sexually reproducing, highly technologically advanced, and warlike humanoid life forms, whose home planet, Niribu, intersects our solar system once every 3,600 years. In antiquity, the "gods" were believed to be immortal. This was not the case. Because the Anunnaki's home planet took 3,600 earth years to orbit the sun, they simply had a different life cycle than humans. This 3,600 year orbit, or cycle, was known as a "divine year," and formally designated a *shar.*[1]

The Anunnaki splashed down in the waters of the Persian Gulf approximately 450,000 years ago (by Zecharia Sitchin's reckoning). These records say that the Anunnaki initially came to Earth on an interplanetary mining expedition, to mine enough gold from Earth to save their home planet's atmosphere. What is wrong with their home planet's atmosphere is never discussed, nor is it ever brought up again in any subsequent texts.

Initially, the earth expedition was led by a commander, engineer, and genetic scientist named Ea ("He whose house is water"). He is also called Enki. Some sources say that Enki was also known as the God of Incantations, partly because of the me (programs, like software—decrees that created civilizations and functions within civilizations in a way that is not clear).

After setting up mission control on Earth, a command center known as E.DIN [in ancient Sumerian meant: "The Abode of the Divine Righteous Ones"] or Dilmun, they began mining gold from the waters of the Persian Gulf. No length of time is given for how long it took to establish the Earth based command center, begin the initial mining operation, and realize that production would be insufficient. Based on other figures that will follow shortly, we estimate that this period was approximately 18,000 Earth years--in Anunnaki time, 5 years, not long in their scheme of time, but long enough to determine that the mission would fail.

From the home planet of Niribu, Enki was reprimanded for failing to meet the gold quota, and his half brother Enlil, also a flight commander, a scientists, and an engineer, was sent to oversee the Earth mining operation. Enlil replaced his half-brother Enki as head of the Earth expedition.

The half brothers did not like each other, as they were in competition to ascend to the throne once their father, Anu, died.

When the half brother Enlil arrived on Earth, it was decided that mining gold in the Persian Gulf would not produce gold fast enough to save the home planet. It was determined that south Africa had the richest deposit of gold on Earth. The marina mining operation was abandoned in favor of mining the pockets of gold found in south Africa.

Why "The Adam" Was Fashioned

The texts state that the Anunnaki flight crew was recruited to do the dirty work of mining the gold in the mines. They reportedly did this for 40 *shars* (144,000 earth years). *"Their toil seemed endless to them, and finally they mutinied."* They refused to work another day in the mines and actually struck.

Commander Enlil, a strict disciplinarian, wanted to execute the mutineers. Enki was for leniency. They argued for days. Finally, it was decided that Enki and Ninhursag (Enki's wife, who was also a genetic scientist) would attempt to "create" a *lulu*; a primitive worker, to take the place of the "gods" in the south African mines.

The Creation of Adamu

The Sumerian texts state how the Anunnaki commander/engineer/genetic scientist, Enki and his wife, Ninhursag, created the first model man. It even mentions the experimental failures:

"Sumerian texts, too, speak of deformed humans created by Enki and the Mother Goddess (Ninhursag, Enki's nurse wife) in the course of their efforts to fashion a perfect Primitive Worker. One text reports that Ninhursag, whose task it was to 'bind upon the mixture the mold of the gods,' got drunk and 'called over to Enki,' 'How good or how bad is Man's body? As my heart prompts me, I can make its fate good or bad.'

"Mischievously, then, according to this text-- but probably unavoidably, as part of a trial and error process--Ninhursag produced a man who could not hold back his urine, a woman who could not bear children, a being who had neither male nor female organs. All in all, six deformed or deficient humans were brought forth by Ninhursag. Enki was held responsible for the imperfect creation of a man with diseased eyes, trembling hands, a sick liver, a failing heart; a second one with sicknesses attendant upon old age; and so on. But finally the perfect Man was achieved—the one Enki named Adapa; the Bible, Adam; our scholars, *Homo sapiens*. This being was so much akin to the gods that one text even went so far as to point out that the Mother Goddess gave to her creature, Man, 'a skin as the skin of a god'--a smooth, hairless body, quite different from that of the shaggy ape-man. [p.348]

-Zecharia Sitchin *(The 12th Planet)*

So according to the ancient texts, Man was created to re-place the Anunnaki flight crew, who had grown weary of work-ing in the south African mines, and had mutinied. Man was, therefore, created as a "Primitive Worker," a gopher (go-for), a being necessary to do the menial tasks that the "gods" felt beneath them. The Adam had been genetically engineered through a series of trial and error experiments that eventually gave Ninhursag and Enki what they were after.

This is how the original text of Genesis (the *Enuma elish*) read before it was edited and renamed Genesis.

The Problem with the Sumerian Texts: Divine Lies

One hundred eighty years ago, our ability to clone or genetically alter human life did not exist. So it is easy to see why scientists rejected this Sumerian account as mythology, especially before its correlations to Genesis had become known. Now that we can perform these same "miracles" of life, this ancient account no longer seems purely mythological. Now that we realize that the genetic engineering of an entire species of beings is possible, we must concede that it could have been done in antiquity.

The scientific feasibility of how humankind was created is indisputable, in the light that we ourselves could now do it. But, even if we buy the "how" of humankind's genetic creation, quite frankly, the "why" stinks. The "why" falls apart with the slightest examination.

Three particularly weak and transparent lies by the "gods" are: 1) That the flight crew actually was needed to work in the mines in south Africa; 2) How Man was created *to replace* the fed up flight crew; 3) Also suspect is the reason for the Earth expedition itself, "to mine enough gold to repair their home planets damaged atmosphere."

Namtar the "Terminator"

The reason the ancient Sumerian texts claiming that the Anunnaki flight crew worked the south African mines and that Man was created to replace them is a transparent lie is because of another story also found in the ancient Sumerian texts. This account narrates how the goddess Inanna/Ishtar went to visit her older sister Ereshkigal, in the Lower World (south Africa). The sisters did not like each other and went into a rage upon seeing each other. Inanna/Ishtar is then killed by her sister's android:

> "No sooner had the two sisters set eyes on each other than both flew into a rage; and Ereshkigal ordered her *Sukka I*Namtar to seize Inanna and afflict her from head to toe. 'Inanna was turned into a corpse, hung from a stake.' Realizing that Inanna was in trouble, Ninshubur rushed from god to god to seek help; but none except Enki could counteract the death-dealing Namtar. His name meant "Terminator;" the Assyrians and Babylonians nick-named him *Memittu*--"The Killer," and Angel of Death.

Unlike the deities or humans, 'he has no hands, he has no feet; he drinks no water, eats no food.'" [p.275]

-Zecharia Sitchin

(*Divine Encounters* 1995)

See the problem? The Anunnaki can create a terrifying, terrible killing machine—an *android--like* Namtar, "whose name meant Terminator," but it never occurs to these highly technologically advanced beings to make an android that could... say...work in the south African mines?

Namtar's mention in the ancient Sumerian texts exposes at least three lies by the "gods": 1) There was NO need for the flight crew to be miners; 2) There was, therefore, NO mutiny from the mines; 3) There was, therefore, NO legitimate reason to create a "Primitive Worker," i.e., No reason to create Man to replace the striking miners.

We're left with the question, *Why did the Anunnaki genetically engineer a "Primitive Worker," if they, didn't really need a "Primitive Worker"?* What fear or motivation would lead the Anunnaki to believe that they must lie to the very creatures they created about why they were created? Certainly, they did not fear the new humans. The new humans thought they were "gods." What then? Were they afraid *for* the new humans?

The Origins Shell Game

If humans were not created to replace the Anunnaki flight crew in the south African mines, why were they created, and why was it necessary to lie about it? Quite simply, the lie was designed to hide exactly when human consciousness came into being. A seemingly esoteric and relatively unimportant point in the larger scheme of things. Yet, nonetheless, that is what the lie has concealed for millenniums-- the true point in time of the origin of the human consciousness.

The Theories of the Origin of the Human Species

There are three dominate theories as to exactly when human life-essences (human consciousness) first came into being: 1) the scientific; 2) the religious; and 3) the metaphysical.

The scientific theory: We have already taken a glimpse at the scientific theory (see Chapters 1 and Chapter 2). The scientific theory is that humans evolved from apes to hominids through various stages until we became as we are today. The problem with the scientific theory is that there are "missing links," gaps, or holes in the continuality of the timeline. If *Homo sapiens* were purely a product of evolution, there should be no "missing links," no unexplainable gaps that produced, as Dr. Diamond called it "The Great Leap Forward." There should be no unexplained spurts in intelligence or technology. Because of these "missing links," the scientific theory of how and when human life-essences first came into being must be labeled incomplete, at best.

The religious theory: The western religious theorists adhere to the belief that God created Adam and Eve in the Garden of Eden. This creation of Adam and Eve in the Garden of Eden, the religious theorists believe, is when human life-essences first came into being, i.e., the origin of the human species and human consciousness. Their source of this belief is the Bible.

As pointed out earlier, Samuel Kramer and Zecharia Sitchin have proved that the biblical books of Genesis are abridged versions of the much older Sumerian texts the *Enuma elish*, and the Sumerian texts were espousing the belief that the Anunnaki were the "gods" who created them.

This misinterpretation, or honest misunderstanding is the heart of the weakness of the religious position. By this we mean that because the source of Genesis was not completely understood, there are several unresolved glitches in its own logic: For instance, the religious theory says that there is/was but one God. And this one God created Adam and Eve. Yet, no biblical scholar of any denomination can explain Genesis' use of the pronouns, "us" and "our," in Genesis 1:26: "And God said, 'Let *us* make man in *our* image, after *our* likeness..:"

Who this singular God is talking to defies all explanation unless, realizing it is an abridged version of the older Sumerian original, we concede that the "us" and "our" are Enki, Ninhursag, Enlil, and the ruling council members of the Anunnaki, "The 12 Who Ruled"(Also known as the *"Elohim"*). Then, and only then does the Genesis texts make sense from the traditional religious interpretation.

So, though well meaning, the religious theory of when human life-essence first came into being does not take into consideration the fact that we are not reading from the original text. Because of this, there are holes it cannot answer in its own supposition.

Another pointed question that defies explanation by the religious theory of the origin of Man is that there is biblical evidence (which we will touch on shortly) that Adam was initially created as an androgynous being--male and female in the same being. The question is simply: Why was Adam created as an androgynous being? The religious theory of the origins of Man has no answer to this seemingly bizarre and illogical question.

The metaphysical theory: The metaphysical theory of when human life- essences first came into being says in essence that the Supreme Being, that had existed before time, before space, before nothingness, in "a void too deep to comprehend," created the universe and cosmos by what amounts to an internal act of Its mind. That is, the universe (or universes) does not exist "outside" of the Creatress/Creator, but within the Creatress/Creator's mind. Therefore, the universe or cosmos and everything in it is made up of the substance of the Mind of the Creatress/Creator, i.e., energy. The universe is patterns of energy shaped by either the mind of the Supreme Being, or by the mind of a woman or a man, or the myriad of creatures inhabiting the dimensions.

The Supreme Being was engaging in what could be considered an act of creative play--or a divine dream. This divine dream took place in stages, building up the dream and the components of the dream as concepts occurred and "grew" from each other, based on recognizable principles like mathematics, music, and consistent physical imperatives--laws.[2]

According to this theory, human consciousness came into being at a point in the evolution of the universe when the

Creator or Creatress became excited about what was transpiring in the evolving universe—human consciousness came into being at about the period when the Creator/Creatress was toying with "a unique new method of reproduction" in *The World Before*, by Ruth Montgomery we read:

> "...Thus began the firmament, and as conditions became ripe on some of the planets, minute forms of life appeared, first propagating by simple fissure (simple cell division) and gradually through more sophisticated methods such as egg and sperm and fetus [sex]. So intricate and exciting became this system of growth that the force we call God desired companionship to share His joy, and in a mighty burst He cast off trillions of sparks from His exalted Being, each spark a soul..."[p.18]
>
> -Ruth Montgomery

According to Ruth Montgomery's guides, human consciousness first came into being at a point in the evolution of the universe when the Creator *wanted to share the excitement of His/Her creation*. No date is given. In earth time, logically, it may have been billions of years ago. That's when human life-essences were created. But this was not the origin of the human species: This theory maintains that the life-forces we may think of as human consciousness existed before the Earth had even cooled.

The key idea is this: If human consciousness (life-essences) first came into being at about the time when life in the universe first began reproducing by means of sexual intercourse, then, logically, the creation of Adam and Eve in a Garden of Eden could not be considered the initial point in time that we came into being. For animals had been reproducing by means of sexual intercourse for millions of years by the time "The Adam" is created.

This "point of entry" issue (of human consciousness) is the heart of the Anunnaki lie. It is what they sought desperately to conceal from the new humans. *When human consciousness first came into being is the real "missing link:"* It is the puzzle piece that makes all the other puzzle pieces fall into place, and begin to make sense.

To fully understand why the Anunnaki lied about "mining gold to repair their home planet's damaged atmosphere," why they lied about working in the mines, mutinying and creating humans to replace the striking worker "gods," it is necessary to turn our UFO/extraterrestrial investigation to the somewhat unscientific words of a psychic--a now dead seer, who, when alive, claimed to be able to read the very skein of the space- time continuum, a medium in reality itself called the "Akashic Records."

We need the dead seer's words because he had the one piece that made all the other pieces to the UFO/extraterrestrial puzzle fit. Without what Edgar Cayce read from the Akashic Records, 60 or 70 years ago, we have only a riddle wrapped in an enigma, as incomprehensible as time travel, and as dark as the Void.

CHAPTER 4:

BEAUTY AND THE BEAST— & THE DARK SECRET

> "The transformation from light astral bodies into solid human bodies is not as difficult as it sounds to earthlings, who originally peopled the earth in just that fashion. They were thought forms in the mind of the Creator, then ethereal souls, then astral bodies and finally in the earth plane they were in solid form."
>
> -Ruth Montgomery's "Guides" on ways "space people" are entering the earth plane (Aliens Among Us)

As mentioned in Chapter 3, the original version of Genesis--the *Enuma elish--the* ancient Sumerian "creation myth"—contained several seemingly harmless lies. These lies were: 1) that the Anunnaki flight crew members were needed to be miners in the south African mines; 2) that the flight crew mutinied from working in the mines; 3) that "The Adam"-- humans—were created to replace the striking flight crew members—humans were created to be "*lulus*"--"primitive workers."

The reason for these lies, as also stated in Chapter 3, was to conceal the original point in time when human consciousness first came into being. It was necessary to convince humans that the creation of Adam and Eve in the Garden of Eden was their first experience in three-dimensional Earth reality. But that was an implicit lie. The race of the Adam was not the first race of humans on the planet Earth. That's what the ancient Sumerian texts was so elaborately crafted to conceal.

For whatever psychological reasons the Anunnaki had deemed necessary, part of the "master plan" hinged on making humans believe that Adam and Eve. were the first humans ever in three-dimensional Earth reality, but this simply was not the case.

We are given two valuable clues that this was not the case in *The Secret Doctrine* (1880), by H.P. Blavatsky. In *The Secret Doctrine*, while describing a creation symbol that looks like the letter "T", Blavatsky states, "It was the glyph of the third root-race to the day of its symbolic Fall--i.e., when the separation of sexes by natural evolution took place." [p. 5] 1) Blavatsky infers that Adam, or the race of Adam, is the *third* root-race. Which means that there were two "root- races" that proceeded Adam; 2) She hints that Adam was androgynous with the statement "the separation of the sexes..."

Adam is Androgynous

Blavatsky only hints, Edgar Cayce is more explicit but they are not the only sources that state that the race of Adam was not the first race of humans in the Earth plane. Nor are they the only sources that claim that the race of Adam were androgynous. There is biblical support for this observation as well: In Genesis 1:27, we read: *"So God created man in his own image, in the image of God created he him; **male and female** created he* *them."* So God creates "Man" in Genesis 1:27--*"male and female created he them.[1]"*

If Adam is not this male AND female being created in Genesis 1:27, why is it necessary to create woman a second time in Genesis 2:22?" And the Lord God said, It is not good that the man should be alone; I will make him a helpmate for him." (Gen. 2:18) "And the rib, which the Lord God had taken from man, made he a woman, and brought her unto the man." (Gen. 2:22)[2] That Adam is a singular, yet dual sexed creature is also implicit in the line: "It is not good that man should be alone." The key word is "alone."

See the problem? Either Adam is an androgynous being, or woman is created twice. From the "alone" statement coming after the "male and female created he them" statement, the logical implication is that Adam is created as male and female-- an androgynous creature, an implication that makes absolutely no sense from present theological understanding of man's origins. Why God would create Adam as an androgynous creature is not even a serious topic of discussion among religious scholars or the clergy. You would not be taken seriously in such a discussion[3].

Yet, the race of Adam being created as androgynous creatures is also a valuable clue to understanding why the "gods" lied about being on expedition to Earth to mine gold, the mutiny, and the bogus reason they give for creating humans.

If Blavatsky and Cayce are correct and the race of the Adam was not the first humans in the Earth plane, why was it necessary to create humans a second (or a third) time? Why was the

Garden of Eden necessary? And how does this answer explain the UFO/extraterrestrial presence, i.e., why they are here?

The Dark Secret

The answer to the question, why is Adam created as an androgynous creature? is the beginning of the understanding of the darkest, longest kept secret in the entirety of human history—bar none. It is an answer that is stranger than science fiction or science fantasy. It is an answer the extraterrestrials labored for millenniums to keep hidden forever. And based on the thoroughness with which humanity's true origins have been obscured, it is very likely that the origin of the human species would have remained an unsolvable enigma forever, if not for a single cryptic passage in an obscure book, by Edgar Cayce, published in 1972, called *The Origin and Destiny of Man.*

Who was Edgar Cayce?

For those of you who have never heard of Edgar Cayce, Cayce (pronounced Cay-cee) was a world-renowned psychic. He was known as the "Sleeping Prophet." Edgar Cayce had the singularly unique ability to put himself into a light hypnotic trance, and accurately diagnose anyone's ailments. His psychic diagnoses were validated by doctors, and they were unfailingly accurate.

These entranced diagnoses were called "readings." These "readings," these attempts· by Cayce to explain the root cause of some incurable or long suffering illness, frequently touched on past life experiences that, according to the entranced Cayce, were often the "karmic" cause of some of the ailments. The ailments were either spiritual lessons to be learned, or karmic debts to be paid.

The degree of accuracy with which Edgar Cayce was able to diagnose people's ailments would by itself seem miraculous. Even today, doctors using the most advanced equipment medical science has to offer cannot boast such accuracy. The feat compounds exponentially when it is understood that it did not matter if the person to be diagnosed was in the same room as Cayce. He could do a "reading" for anyone, if told that person's name and where she or he would be at the time of the reading, even if they were thousands of miles away!

Every one of Cayce's over 14,000 "readings" were recorded and are on file at the Edgar Cayce Foundation in Virginia Beach, Virginia.

Someone got the idea to ask the "voice" that spoke through the entranced Edgar Cayce what exactly was its source of information and how did it know these things. The "voice" said that it read from what is known as the "Akashic Records," or a medium in reality itself that keeps a lasting (eternal) impression of every thought, every word and every deed that has ever been spoken, thought, or acted upon. The voice said that biblically the Akashic Records are called The Book of God's Remembrance, or The Judgment Book

At some point when Edgar Cayce was alive, the "voice" was asked to tell what it knew (could read from the Akashic Records) about the creation of the universe, including humanity's origins.

The Pre-Adam Humans

Cayce says, in essence, that after the Creator gave off the "burst of exaltation that created trillions of life-essences," some of these life-essences stayed close to the Creator; some explored other worlds or other dimensions or other universes; some found their way to Earth. These initial life-essences were points of self-aware consciousness, embodied in light. Aware of their existence and of the Creator.

Because these human life-essences were still in a somewhat higher vibrational realm, they could only watch the activities of the animals and other life-forms evolving on the planet Earth. They saw the animals having sex, they saw them eating, they saw the oceans, the rivers, the warm tropical settings, the wild growing fruits, and plants, and became obsessed with finding a way to experience three-dimensional Earth reality. This was NOT part of the Creator's plan.

These new human life-essences were so enchanted and enthralled by what they saw that eventually they tried an experiment: They attempted to "project" their consciousness into the bodies of the animals they had been observing and attempting to influence telepathically. This they were eventually able to do, and through these projections of their consciousness, they were able to experience three-dimensional Earth reality--to a degree.

Soon, however, the game of projecting their consciousness and experiencing sex or eating through the animals was no longer gratifying. Perhaps the consciousness of the animals "muffled" or in some way distorted the experience. At any rate, the game shifted into a higher, much more dangerous level. At this new level of the game, the human life- essences learned to playfully create "thought-form" bodies--visualizations--mental images of bodies whose form or shape they could "hold" together with the sheer power of their god-like minds and will.

These "dream-bodies" took whatever form the human life-essences fancied. Whatever they could imagine--winged serpents, dragons, unicorns, centaurs, satyrs, sphinx, griffins, mermaids, giant half insect half human monstrosities--they could and did become. If the body needed wings, they would simply imagine wings. If it needed scales, they would imagine scales, etc. From this level of their divine creativity, they dreamed up bodies they thought would be "fun" to inhabit. They then projected these dream-bodies into three-dimensional Earth reality, and in this way experienced sex, eating, and all the sensations of Earth existence directly.

Sex was the number one lure. Sensations. Tasting. Eating. Running. Flying. Swimming. Sensations. Their mental and creative mind powers were vast. They were sparks from the Creator, with all the power implicit in that source. They were like children fascinated with a new toy, the awesome creative powers of their own minds. In this beginning, there was no overt malice. It was simply a game, and the desire to experience another dimension.

Lilith

The very first human life-essence that attempted this "dream-body" thought projection into three dimensional earth reality was a life-essence that chose to thought project as a female entity. (In the higher vibrational realms, life-essences are sexless—neither male nor female.) Her name was Lilith, and she thought-projected as a naked, human-looking woman, with "wings and bird-like feet." She was an eerie, owl-like creature. Jewish legend holds that she howled or screeched in the night.

In the Cayce texts we read:

> The first female was called Lilith, the fore runner of Eve, and a conglomeration of monstrosities emerged. The Cyclops, the satyr, centaur, unicorn, and various forms mentioned in mythology, having animal bodies and human heads, came into existence. Thus the souls who had been hovering about, influencing and directing, inhabited bodies which were projections of their own mental creations—and propagated a race of monstrosities. Their bodies were their own creations, not God's. These were the "daughters of men, the giants in the earth," of the Old Testament. So a weird, corrupt state of existence came into being..."
>
> -Edgar Cayce
> (The Origin and Destiny of Man--1972)

Thousands of other human life-essences followed projecting as male "dream-bodied" monstrous creatures. They had sex with Lilith and with the animals, "in a cave near the Red Sea."

No Way Home

There is no mention of how long this dream-body thought projection cosmic mind game continued. Whether years, decades, centuries, or eons, Cayce does not say. But disaster, apparently, came slowly: The way the game had gone was that the human life- essences would project their consciousness into the dream-bodies, then project into three-dimensional earth reality. They would enjoy sex, eating, feel the ground under their hooves, the sensation of flight, wind under their wings, etc. Then, once bored, or out of an instinctive caution, they would abandon the dream-bodies by simply releasing their mental hold on them and return to the higher vibrational realms.

Eventually, either through laziness or because they grew careless and began to believe that there was nothing to fear, they would stay for longer and longer periods in the dream-bodies, in three-diminsional earth reality. This was their great mistake. Gradually, at first imperceptibly, the more they partook of food and sex and other sensations in the 3rd dimension, the more their dream-bodies congealed and hardened. This change must have taken place so gradually that, at first, no change was even noticeable. However, after an extended period of time, to what must have been their great surprise and terror, they discovered that they could no longer dissolve the dream- bodies. They could not mentally release them, and therefore, could not return to the higher vibrational realms.

This was the entrapment, and Cayce says this was the "original sin," this tampering with the Creator's plan.

This period of bizarre entrapment lasted for hundreds of thousands of years. During this period, the human life-essences trapped in the dream-bodies gradually began to forget what they once were, divine beings from a higher dimensional realm. They began to believe that they were the dream- bodied creatures they saw reflected in pools or bodies of water. As their memories deteriorated, so did their divine intelligence. They became, for all practical purposes, what they had pretended to be, i.e., no smarter than any insect or animal or bird or fish that creped or crawled or walked the Earth, flew the skies, or swam in the seas.

There had been life-essences who had not participated in the projected consciousness game, who had kept an eye on the plight of those who had attempted it. They had noted that without even self-awareness of who they once had been, the hybrid creatures would be lost forever in a dimension that they would never have the intelligence to understand and never be able to find their way out of.

The short, cryptic passage that refers to the cosmic rescuers was this:

"Amilius, with the aid of spiritual-minded soul entities from other realms—the 'sons of the Most High'-- intervened in this miss happened evolution which earth-man had created for himself.

From among the various physical forms on earth a body was patterned which most perfectly fitted the needs of man. This was a body that would help, not hinder, in the struggle for at-one-ment (atonement) with the Maker. By his own choice, Amilius himself descended into matter and became Adam, man as flesh and blood, the first of the perfect race, the first of the Sons of God as opposed to the *Daughters of Men*,' the freakish offspring of the

Mixtures. This was the reason for the admonishment to *'keep the race pure,'* for *'the sons of God looked upon the daughters of Men and saw them as being air.'"* (Gen.6:2).

-Edgar Cayce
(The Origin and Destiny of Man--1972)

Though unnamed, it is obvious that the cosmic rescuers are extraterrestrials. Note the even more cryptic reference to the genetic creation of Adam:

"From among the various physical forms on earth a body was patterned which most perfectly fitted the needs of man."

-Edgar Cayce - *The Origin and Destiny of Man*, 1972

This cosmic mind game turned tragedy was man's pre-Adam excursion and experience in three-dimensional earth reality. This dream-body thought-form projection entrapment in three-dimensional earth reality was why it was necessary to genetically "fashion" a human species, since human consciousness or human life-essences existed long before the creation of the human species. This excursion was the beginning, not the creation of Adam and Eve, in the Garden of Eden.

As for the anomalies in the scientific timeline, these maybe subtle points in time at which there has been either overt or discrete intervention in humankind's evolution.

Human life-essences existed in three-dimensional earth reality before the Anunnaki genetically engineered "the Adam."

47

That is why in the ancient Sumerian texts Adam is called "The Prototype," "The Model Man"--or more precisely a pattern man--a blueprint man, to create others like the prototype.

The genetic fashioning of the prototype Adam was the answer to the question, "What safe homogeneous form can we transfer the consciousness of the entrapped ones into?"

CHAPTER 5:

FABRICATING HISTORY, THE ART OF THE LIE: &
THE MISSING *FIRST BOOK OF ENOCH*

A very subtle piece of empirical evidence in the investigation of UFOs, extraterrestrials and whether or not these hybrid creatures actually existed is a nagging question that permeated this entire research effort. The more connections and puzzle pieces that began to fit, the more pronounced became this nagging, unsettling, underlying question. That question was: Why did they leave us these clues? Why not either omit ALL of the "sensitive" information, or why not simply lie about everything? Why tell us any of the things, even in coded or cryptic form, that might draw attention to a possible cover-up?

After considering this question for some time, and after trying to envision the thinking processes of these beings that genetically engineered humans or possibly the humans that edited the books of the Bible, it became apparent that we may never fully understand their decision to leave clues.

Perhaps, they hoped that we would one day learn the entire truth. Then again, perhaps, they had no choice. By this we mean, perhaps, the only choices they had were what bits of truth they would code or encrypt and mix in with what omissions and with what outright lies. We surmise this based on the observation that the best lies--the believable lies--are the ones that have at least some truth in them.

A Thought Experiment

That observation alone is hardly sufficient to base an entire premise on. So we performed a thought experiment: Let's say it's the year 2019A.D. A small group of international genetic scientists have been given unlimited funding and government sanctions to produce a few hundred highly intelligent, multi-ethnic, very strong, superhuman clones (a "limited edition" series).

One of the project's objectives is that the clones should not be aware that they are clones. The scientists want the clones to mix with the various populations of various countries, marry, and produce a sub-race of half-clone half-human children, who would also be studied by the project's scientists.

You don't want the clones to know that they are clones is your primary psychological objective. What do you tell them is their history? Their origin? If you give this psychological problem some thought, you will discover that there are really only four possible scenarios in regard to what you will tell the clones is their history:

1.) **You could tell them absolutely nothing.** Give them no history. When they ask, you shrug your shoulders, or do something equally infuriating. Your silence will, of course, excite curiosity. The clones will begin researching their origins.

2.) **You could tell them a complete lie or lies.** When they ask, you tell them their parents died in a car accident. You must be prepared to fabricate histories for these non-existent parents, for relatives, grandparents, uncles and aunts, and *their* histories. If any element of the histories seems inconsistent, the whole lie could fall apart, and the clones would begin investigating their true origins.

3.) You could tell them the complete truth. When they ask, you tell them they were genetically created in a secret laboratory on an unnamed military installation, in the Nevada desert, and, of course, completely compromise the project's prime psychological objective.

4.) You could tell them a combination of believable lies, omissions, and cryptic half-truths that will *resonate* a degree of truth to both their conscious and subconscious minds. This account, however, must *feel* true. If it does, and because there is *some* truth in it, it would be more readily accepted than scenarios 1, 2, or 3. The inconsistencies or the contradictions could then be explained as the mysterious ways of the Supreme Being.

Suspicions would be raised with fabricating histories based on premises 1 through 3. Only choice 4 would quell suspicion. Only choice 4 could withstand the onslaught of the endless waves of questions that would be asked by a naturally curious species. With choice 4, some clones would still investigate, but most would be sold (or conclude that there is no God, based on inconsistencies, and so, not search or investigate the fabricated history, which would serve your purpose equally as well).

That's why we believe they left clues. That was the only way to psychologically sell the cover-up—omit some, lie some, tell some cryptic truths, to make it believable. Their only choices, we believe, that would not draw suspicion, was what to omit, what to outright lie about, and what bits of truth to encode and embed in the tale.

We surmise that from such a paradigm the ancient Sumerian texts and the books of Genesis were edited, either by the Anunnaki, the clergy (the Levite priests), or both.

Omit Some

The exact dates or chronology of what happened when, in the *Enuma elish* (ancient Sumerian texts), is a good example of this. For instance, there are no dates given in the ancient Sumerian texts. Not even approximations, and there is a fundamental inconsistency with a race of highly technologically advanced extraterrestrial beings, who were capable of calculating Earth time in derivatives of 3,600 units, who invented the first solar and lunar calendars, determined the exact day of the Earth's equinox (the day when there are exactly the same number of hours in the night as in the day)[1] yet conveniently include no dates of the key events in their narrative of the creation of humans. Not a one.

Which leaves us to conclude that "chronology" was one of the selected choices in what to purposefully omit.

In *The 12th Planet*, Zecharia Sitchin has put together a chronology of the Anunnaki's Earth expedition. Through various methods, which Zecharia attests to, he confidently places the date of their splash down at 450,000 years ago. Zecharia Sitchin's chronology of the Anunnaki's Earth expedition and the puzzle pieces we have found add up to an interesting coincidence.

The Chronology

Consider:

- **450,000 years ago:** Zecharia Sitchin is positive, the Anunnaki splashed down in the waters of the Persian Gulf. He's got documentation from 3 or 4 sources that proves this.[2]

- **18,000 years ago:** The ancient Sumerian texts do not give a duration of how long it took the Anunnaki to set up a base of operation after their landing, "begin mining gold in the waters of the Persian Gulf," and decide that this was a bad idea. We estimate that it took 18,000 earth years--5 of their years (not long in their scheme of time-- *shars*) to setup a base of operation, build an Earth based command center (E.DIN, or Dilmun), survey the planet, map meteorological and geological patterns, investigate the dangers of the animal and plant life on the planet, set up equipment, communications, and operating procedures. (This estimate is based on the amount of time not accounted for from the 450,000 year ago splashdown, minus the 144,000 years mining gold in south African mines, minus a DNA backdating variable we will disclose shortly.)

- **144,000 earth years** "mining gold in south African mines." The only time approximation we are given is how long the Anunnaki flight crew spent mining gold before they mutinied. That this 144,000 earth years spent mining gold in south African mines is the only time approximation we are given in the creation myth is curious. Do they want us to focus on it? You bet. It's the old, "Nothing up my sleeve" routine, or, "Can we get a volunteer from the audience?", i.e., They want us to focus on the 144,000 years spent "mining gold in south African mines" because they do have something up their sleeves.

Timeout: The 144,000 earth years (40 *shars*) the Anunnaki flight crew spent mining gold in south African mines is another lie we catch them in. This is not to say that they did not actually mine gold in south Africa. We're relatively sure they did. Both Sumerian and Egyptian inscriptions indicated that they did. But they did it because they needed a "cover story," some seemingly harmless activity to put in the records. But it was just "cover." Camouflage. Like police or government agents pretending to fix some bad cables across the street from a stakeout. If anyone sees the agents or police while on stakeout, they figure they're just some poor stiffs that had to work overtime. Cover.

So, the Anunnaki did some mining so that it could be said (and written later) that "they did some mining." They needed some overt reason to be on expedition to Earth. If all went well, there would be some very intelligent, very inquisitive humans down the road that would read about this time and would question every word, every syllable, every symbol contained in the ancient texts left by the "gods." These intelligent humans would question everything the texts said the "gods" said or did. So the "damaged home planet atmosphere, mining gold to fix it up" was the cover story they went with. Not a bad cover story considering that it has survived for many millenniums unquestioned or believed to be simply mythology. But it was just fluff. Smoke. Misdirection.

What were the Anunnaki really doing for 144,000 earth years (40 *shars*), if not mining gold in south African mines? The missing *First Book of Enoch* (from the Bible) is the prime clue.

The Book of the "Watchers"

The First Book of Enoch never made it into the Bible. For some mysterious reason it was edited out. We only heard of its existence through the writings of the religious historian Professor Elaine Pagels, in her book *The Origins of Satan*. In this religious historical investigation to determine at what point in history did the church start espousing belief in a devil, there is mention of another mysterious book called *The Book of the Watchers*. In *The Origins of Satan*, Professor Pagels explains the essence of *The Book of the Watchers*:

> "*The Book of the Watchers*, a collection of visionary stories, is set, in turn, into a larger collection called *The First Book of Enoch*. It tells how the "watcher" angels, who God appointed to supervise ("watch over") the universe, fell from heaven. Starting from the story of Genesis 6,

in which the 'sons of God' lusted for human women, this author combines two different accounts of how the watchers lost their heavenly glory.

The first describes how Semihazah, leader of the watchers, coerced two hundred other angels to join him in a pact to violate divine order by mating with human women. These mismatches produced a race of bastards, the giants known as *Nephilim* ["fallen ones"],' from whom there were to proceed demonic spirits, 'who brought violence upon earth and devoured its people...'

The Book of the Watchers says pointedly that these greedy monsters 'consumed the produce of all the people until the people hated feeding them, the monsters then turned directly to 'devour the people.'"

-Elaine Pagels *(The Origin of Satan)*

How Professor Pagels gained access to the book she does not say. The significant point is that there was a book that was a chronology of a group of "angels" that had been commanded to supervise (to "watch over") the universe. It states how 200 of these angels, plus their leader Semihazah, "fell from heaven." But it's just a euphemism, i.e., more code.--According to Zecharia Sitchin, in *The 12th Planet*, the "angels" were the flight crew members, and they didn't "fall" from grace, they mutinied. They mutinied not from the mines in south Africa, but from their post as flight crew members aboard spacecraft orbiting Earth.³ They mutinied because they "lusted for sex with human women." According to this account, their sexual intercourse with the human women resulted in the birth of "giants," and monsters known as *Nephilim*⁴ ["fallen ones"].

Why *The First Book of Enoch* Never Made It into The Bible

The existence of *The Book of the Watchers* and its contents is a contradiction to the "mining for gold in south African mines" cover-story. The flight crew didn't mutiny from the mines, they mutinied from their post. That's why *The First Book of Enoch* was omitted. It created an unwanted second version of what happened. A glaring contradiction to the official cover-story.

The omission of *The First Book of Enoch* (containing *TheBook of the Watchers)* from the Bible is evidence supporting the theory of what we believe the Anunnaki really did during those 144,000 earth years they claimed to be mining gold.

If Not Mining Gold, What?

If this is a real problem, and not mythology, and these beings (the Anunnaki) are really going to make the effort to resolve it, what would be the first thing that they would do? Put the mythology thinking aside. If this is a real problem, how are they going to solve this problem of human life-essences (human consciousness) trapped in congealed thought-form projections?

As scientists attempting to find a solution to an extremely unique and complex problem, what is the first thing ANY scientist would do? Rush in there and fix the problem? Get those trapped human life-essences out? Draw up a plan of action? Confer with the other senior members of the flight crew for solutions? Jump in there and do something?! Not likely.

The first thing any scientist would do, when faced with an enormous unknown—a unique problem that perhaps no one has ever attempted to solve, or that perhaps, has no solution--is to study it! A scientist would want to gather all of the data, all the pertinent facts that she or he could, before attempting anything. There was too much at stake. Too many things could go wrong without first discovering the heart of the problem, then mapping out a strategy or the steps of a solution. Which brings us back to *The First Book of Enoch* and why it was omitted from the Bible. It was the use of the term "watchers." It was too suggestive—gave too much away.

They were called "watcher" angels because they were scientists and flight crew members observing a problem, searching for a solution--"watchers." Watching, observing, gathering data, and analyzing this information. The Sumerian name for them was I.GI.GI ["Those who watch"]. They were watching the mixtures, or hybrid creatures; studying their life cycles; their eating habits; their social structure; their sexual habits and preferences; their level of intelligence, etc.

That the Anunnaki spent 40 *shars* (144,000 earth years) studying the problem would be a logical first step. The idea that they were "gods," and simply swooped down from heaven after the decision to make Man, then made Man, is the myth they wanted to perpetuate. Perhaps, they wanted the new humans to believe in something, so they decided to maintain the illusion that they were "gods," as long as possible. Better to have the humans believe in something, rather than in nothing. Better to have the humans believe that they were "gods," than to try to explain the concept of an "Omnipresent, Eternal, Boundless, and Immutable PRINCIPLE, on which all speculation is impossible, since it transcends the power of human conception and could only be dwarfed by any human expression or similitude"-- the "Rootless Root of all that was, is or ever shall be.

So, where were we?

a. **450,000 years ago** the Anunnaki splashed down in the waters of the Persian Gulf.
b. **-18,000 years** to set up a base of operations, survey the planet, get situated.
c. **-144,000 earth years** (40 *shars*) studying the problem and searching for a solution.

> 450,000 -- landed on Earth
> -18,000 -- setup operations
> -144,000 -- "watching" gathering data
> _____
> 288,000 -- DNA backdating places Adam here.

We derived the -18,000 years to set up a base of operation by assuming that the DNA backdating of when Adam actually existed is somewhat accurate. *DNA backdating places the actual appearance of "Adam" at approximately 288,000 years ago,* which coincides with the chronology derived from the ancient

Sumerian "creation myth" texts. DNA backdating places Eve at 250,000 to 275,000 years ago-[6]

Take the splash down date 450,000 years ago, then subtract the time it took to set up operations-18,000 years; then subtract the observing, information gathering, looking for a solution period of -144,000 years. By then, the Anunnaki had all their ducks in a row, and decided to go for it—they then began the genetic experiments that "fashioned" "The Adam," "The Prototype Man."

Ironically, this was only the beginning of their problems. This first "race of Adam" (the "sons of God") turned out to be some what of a failure. These were the androgynous humans. That may be why there's a gap between DNA backdating placing Adam at 288,000 years ago, and archaeologists placing the anatomically fully modern *Australopithecus Africanus* (the southern African ape) at approximately 100,000 years ago. The androgynous race of humans were genetically fashioned, lived, and became extinct in the gap between 288,000 years ago and 100,000 years ago.

There is an admitted period here when there seems to exist virtually no records of either the Anunnaki's activity, or any trace of humans of any kind (250,000? years ago to 100,000 years ago). The Anunnaki may have been regrouping during this period. We surmise that the appearance of *Australopithecus Africanus* (the "south African ape," with the fully modern anatomy) was the genetic evidence that the Anunnaki had wiped the slate clean and were starting over again from a new paradigm, i.e., a new model man.

Blavatsky says that her Indian sources for *The Secret Doctrine* called the race of Adam the 3rd root race. They said that we are the 5th root race (not ethnic, but as a species). Could the *Australopithecus Africanus,* Neanderthal, Cro-Magnons, etc. have been the 4th root race of the human species, and the hybrid creatures the 2nd root race?

CHAPTER 6:
THE DILEMMA OF THE GODS
WHY ADAM WAS ANDROGYNOUS

"For at first the sons of God, the souls, were androgy-nous, combining male and female as one."

-Edgar Cayce
(*The Origin & Destiny of* Man--1972)

Breaking the Genesis Codes

The Edgar Cayce material was a virtual biblical Rosetta Stone giving us the decoded meaning of several key phrases and ideas hidden in the books of Genesis. We may never fully understand why these clues were given. Either coded or cryptic truths add believability to a cover-story, or, perhaps, the Anunnaki wanted to see if we would ever evolve sufficiently to decipher the code and glimpse the dark secret of our beginning.

Whatever the reason, let's look at the clues they left us, and how the Genesis texts are, at least in part, a chronicle of the deeper story of why Adam was genetically engineered as an an-drogynous creature. This reason is also a large part of what was hidden. Revealed, it is further proof that *Homo sapiens* are a ge-netically engineered species. It also validates the flesh and blood reality of the hybrid creatures--the beings we have believed for millenniums to be only entertaining mythology or legend.

Genesis Decoded

The Genesis texts reads:

"That the sons of God saw the daughters of men that they were fair; and took them wives of all which they chose." (Gen. 6:2)

The Cayce account says that "daughters of men" was the biblical code name for the mixtures--the entrapped ones--the unicorns, the dragons, the satyrs, the mermaids, the giants, etc. It said that "sons of God" was the biblical code name for the newly genetically engineered race of the Adam. "Sons of God" was actually a play on words, for the "sons of God" were the literal genetic offspring of the Anunnaki, created from the ovum of female apes and the genetic code of selected flight crew members of the Anunnaki Earth expedition[1].

Within the Genesis texts itself, we are given a mere hint that the race of Adam were androgynous beings in the short phrase-- *"male and female created he them."*(Gen. 1:27) In *The Origin and Destiny of Man*, Cayce comes right out and says as much:

"For at first the sons of God, the souls, were androgynous, combining male and female as one."

So, the initial race of Adam were created as androgynous creatures. Why? Why androgynous creatures? In the entire Bible, that the race of Adam was initially created as androgynous beings (a somewhat significant point) is given this single, unclear sentence. Again, the deeper mystery is not that this was glossed over, but why wasn't it simply omitted? Why give us this clue at all?

Why it was not simply omitted we cannot say. But to understand why Adam was initially created as an androgynous creature is to glimpse the dark secret of humanity's origins, something neither the Anunnaki nor the Levite priests wanted.

Let's read the passage again with the keys Cayce provided in understanding the code words and phrases and see what we get: Inserting our new understanding we get:

"The newly genetically engineered race of androgynous humans saw the unicorns, dragons, satyrs, mermaids, sphinx, etc. that they were fair; and took them wives of all which they chose."

Since marriage had not yet been invented, we may assume that "took them wives of all which they chose" is a euphemism for they had rampant sex with whomever they wanted. We then get:

"The newly created androgynous race of the Adam saw the unicorns, dragons, satyrs, mermaids, sphinx, etc, that they were fair; and took them wives of all which they chose."

Another subtle hint that this passage is referring to androgynous creatures is that the race of Adam are called ONLY "sons of God." Not "sons and daughters of God," but just "sons of God." Were there only sons? No. We believe this is a subtle hint that the "race of Adam" were all of this same bi-sexual, androgynous nature. The androgynous beings were only referred to by the male portion of their sex as a misdirection ploy we will explain in the next chapter. Thus they were all called the "sons of God."

The Frustration of the "Gods"

If we carefully examine the implications of each of the coded references, the reason Adam is created as androgynous can be deduced from the information contained within this very biblical chapter. For later in this chapter (Gen. 6), it is revealed that this blatant loose sexual behavior was one of the main reasons the "Lord" was contemplating the destruction of humans:

"There were giants in the earth in those days; and also, after that, when the sons of God came in unto the daughters of men, and they bear children to them..." (Gen.6:4)

"And God saw that the wickedness of man was great in the earth... And it repented the Lord that he had made man on the earth, and it grieved him at his heart. And the Lord said, I will destroy man whom I have created from the face of the earth, both man, and beast, and the creeping thing, and the fowls of the air; for it repented me that I have made them." (Gen. 6:5 - 6:7)

There is a commonsense logic inconsistency here. If this is actually God—the Almighty Supreme Being—creating man in these passages, then how is it possible that God cannot anticipate the race of Adam's sexual behavior? How could God make anything and not know what its nature would be, and still consider Himself God? That's one of those inconsistencies that causes careful readers of the Bible to conclude that there really is no God. It is not inconsistent if we realize that the beings that genetically engineered the Adam were not "gods." Though highly technologically advanced, they didn't know everything. They made their calculations, then took their best shot.

But that's a digression. The point is they've given us more code in this passage, and more clues. It's not really God, it's the Anunnaki high command, probably Enki under his guise as Yahweh. If we read the passage with that understanding, we get:

"I [/we] will destroy man, i.e., the androgynies, whom I [/we] have genetically engineered from the face of the earth; both man (the androgynies), and beast, and the creeping thing..."

We've got a pinch of untruth in this passage--misdirection. It is implied that the "Lord" made all of the creatures named in this verse. That is the untruth. That the creatures named were NOT made by any god is why they so infuriated the "Lord."

By "beast" the "Lord"/the Anunnaki high command is not referring to Bambi, the woodland creature, or her friends the bears in the forest, or the other naturally occurring creatures on the planet Earth. The tipoff is the use of the phrase "the creeping thing." (One can almost hear and feel the utter distain in those printed words "the creeping thing.") Does the "Lord" not know the names of all His creatures? He DOESN'T know the name of this one because it is NOT one of his creations (i.e., not a naturally occurring creature). In this passage, "beast, and the creeping thing², and the fowls of the air are subtle references to the "daughters of men," the centaurs, satyrs, the serpent-like half-human half-snake creatures, and the flying monstrosities, etc.

The translation of this coded passage is that the "Lord" [the Anunnaki] intends to kill the androgynies and the daughters of men for their rampant sex with each other, and because these sexual unions were creating more monstrosities and more giants—more of the very problem they were trying to resolve. The chapter slides nicely into the tale of Noah and the Ark, but that is simply more misdirection. The duration between these events may have been dramatically shortened. A true scientist is not so eager to throw in the towel with an experiment that has taken 40 years of his life to reach fruition. He may be in a state of utter rage over the turn of events, but he'll be searching for a way to salvage the project, if he or she can. Logically, this should have been the next disclosure. But the preamble to what the "Lord" decides to do does not appear until Isaiah 34, a biblical book that hardly anyone has ever heard of, and even fewer people have actually read, i.e., a good place to hide a valuable clue.

Exactly how do these passages demonstrate why the race of Adam was genetically engineered as androgynous? Those biblical passages record what had been a monumental, heroic effort by the "gods." But an effort that had none the less failed. Partly because these beings were not "gods;" partly because they may have needed to record the events for their own gratification; partly because they may have hoped that we would one day evolve far enough to decipher the codes and truly appreciate the sacrifices they made, in the light of the fact that they were not "gods," they had to record this event. If for no other reason than the sheer magnitude of this tragic effort and that it showcased the heart of the entrapment and the human dilemma. It was a story that had to be told in some form or fashion. (At least, that's our theory.)

The Failure of the "Gods"

What had happened was this: After studying the problem for 144,000 earth years (40 of their years), after probably endless meetings think-tanking the problem, debating the best course of actions, the best body type, etc., after studying the psychology of the mixtures, their sexual habits, eating habits, life cycles, rate of mortality, nature of offspring, tracking the migration of the life- essence after death, after numerous genetic experiments and at least eight failed genetic attempts, and after finally deciding on the most logical genetic prototype for a "safe vessel" for the entrapped hybrid creatures to incarnate into, after genetically producing the androgynous Adam--(Anunnaki women actually carrying the experimental human zygotes 10 months to term, in their own wombs, and after actually birthing the new humans--androgynous and hideous as they must have seemed to the Anunnaki women), there were two major failures:

1. Adam had been created as a *self- reproducing* androgynous being in the hope that the androgynous beings would not desire sex with the animals and with the mixtures[4]. This was the heart of the initial master plan. *This was the reason the race of Adam was created as androgynous creatures.* The four-handed four-footed bodies were not a form of punishment. Since the hybrids were weird, bizarre looking creatures, some with many heads, many arms, animal, insect, bird, fish, or fantasy bodies, the Anunnaki reasoned that based on the dream-bodies they had initially chosen, these life-essences would feel right at home in a body with four arms and four legs. They reasoned that this would be desirable to the trapped souls.

Your Place or Mine?

The questions may be asked: Why was this so important? Why were the Anunnaki so concerned with the sexual habits of the race of the Adam that they would genetically create the race of Adam as androgynous creatures, with four hands and four feet, that could sexually self-reproduce? Did they feel that sex with hybrid creatures and animals was perverse? Morally wrong? Or was there some deeper reason for their alarm at this behavior?

There is biblical evidence in the books of Leviticus and Isaiah (which we will touch on in Chapter 8) that indicate that they did feel it was perverse and morally wrong. The Anunnaki said of these human-hybrid sexual unions that "It is confusion," and they warned humans "not to defile" them-selves in that way. But there were also deeper, more practi-cal considerations. In the Anunnaki analysis of the situation, probably one of the early conclusions they arrived at during those 40 *shars* of observing the problem was that they felt, be-sides the human/animal/creature sexual unions being "confu-sion," that the root cause of the enchantment and entrapment had been the fascination with, desire for, and participation in sexual intercourse with the animals and with other hybrid creatures. They may have felt that the mental focus and the highly charged emotional state of lust was the primary reason that kept the hybrid creatures focused in three-dimensional earth reality and trapped in the dream-bodies more than any other factor. (Cayce also states sex as one of the main causes of the initial entrapment.)

In the hybrids (the mixtures), the Anunnaki perceived a weird species of sex addicts. It wasn't that the Anunnaki were against sex. They seemed to enjoy it quite frequently in the ancient Sumerian texts with their own mothers, sisters, daugh-ters, and granddaughters. But they weren't trapped in freakish dream-bodies either. (In the ancient Sumerian texts, there was never any mention of genetic defects caused by this inter-fam-ily breeding.) So perhaps they felt justified in having this duel standard. Plus, their sexual adventures, for the most part, didn't involve other species.[5] They tended to have sexual intercourse with only other humanoid life forms. They may have felt that multiple species sexual intercourse (and breeding) was an abomination of the laws of nature.

Therefore, their primary focus was not just on how to free the human consciousness from the freakish congealed dream bodied forms, but once that feat had been some how accomplished, the equally or more important task became how to alter the mental focus of the sex addicted human consciousness' so that they would not create some equal or greater sexual folly, once in a different guise, i.e., they had to get the human life-essences' minds off sex with the animals and the mixtures at all cost, or the mission would fail no matter what else they were able to accomplish. Thus, Adam is initially genetically engineered as a self-reproducing androgynous being.

These considerations would have been a major part of the rescue plan, and a contributing factor in the decision to create the race of Adam as androgynies. But after all that painstaking planning, preparation, and millenniums of analysis of the psychology of these creatures and other problems of entrapment, they were wrong on just about everything, especially the sexual psychology part. When the Bible said that:

"That the sons of God saw the daughters of men that they were fair; and they took them wives of all which they chose."

That biblical passage is actually an abbreviated, coded reference to this monumental error in judgment. It is a humongous understatement that is really recording this unanticipated failure by the Anunnaki. *The androgynous race of Adam was not supposed to desire sex with any other creatures—not even with other androgynous beings like itself*. Yet, what the Anunnaki observed was that, even though Adam could self-reproduce, the androgynous Adam humans (the "sons of God") still desired sex with the animals and mixtures, and probably other androgynous beings, i.e., the 144,000 year old plan had failed miserably. All that work. All that planning. All those wasted years. It seemed that nothing the Anunnaki could do could break the race of Adam's sexual addiction.[7]

With the genetic creation of Adam, they had managed to free the human life-essences from the congealed dreambody entrapment. That part of the mission had been a success. However, the rest of the master plan had failed. They had under estimated the degree of sexual addiction. After this major effort had mostly failed, they hadn't really contemplated a Plan B. Not knowing how to proceed, angry that the new race of Adam did not understand the magnitude of its folly, frustrated beyond human comprehension, can you understand why the "Lord" was ready to go nuclear and destroy the entire newly genetically created race of the Adam now? They had terribly misjudged the sexual psychology of the androgynous race of the Adam, and nobody likes to be that wrong.

So, the first major failure of the mission was that producing Adam as a creature that could self-reproduce DID NOT curtail the desire for sex with the animals and mixtures. That's what that passage is a chronology of. It also demonstrates that the Genesis texts had been, at least in part, obscured to hide any errors or mistakes committed by the "gods." If it were realized that the "gods" had made such a monumental blunder, no one would believe they were "gods."

2. The second unforeseen failure was another major miscal-culation by the Anunnaki in understanding the psychology of the race of Adam. The clue to this miscalculation comes from a quote found in Erich Von Daniken's *Gods From Outer Space?* Von Daniken quotes Plato's *Symposium:*

> "Originally there was a third sex in addition to the male and female sexes. This human had four hands and four feet... great was the strength of these humans, their minds were presumptuous, they planned to storm heaven and lay violent hands on the gods."

Implicit in this quote from Plato's *Symposium* is that the androgynous race of Adam did not like the four-handed, four-footed bodies that the "gods" had fashioned for them. And they intended to get even with the "gods," if they could.

Given the major failure of not being able to curtail the sexual perversions of the race of Adam, and the fact that not only were the race of Adam not responding as predicted, but did not even like the forms that the Anunnaki had chosen for them, eventually, the Anunnaki did throw in the towel. Why not scrap this first attempt and start over from a new paradigm? This may have been when Eve was created. When it was decided to "split" the life-essences into separate male and female entities, and to make humans look more anatomically like the "gods."[8]

There are some sources that claim that this split was not simply one of gender. That the Anunnaki split the life-essences themselves, so that the new humans would yearn for union with their very selves. Not a metaphor, but the theory is that somewhere there is a human that is the literal other part of your self.

There was another problem with the Genesis texts. After the "Lord" stated His displeasure with the race of the Adam in Gen. 6:5-6:7, Genesis goes into the story of Noah and the Ark. There is a logical, natural progression in introducing the story of Noah and the Ark here because the "Lord" decides to send the flood to destroy Man in the Noah and the Ark tale. But the transition from the "Lord's" grievous mood to the story of the flood still seems choppy. Forced. Like something is missing.

After the "Lord" shows his displeasure with the race of Adam, what should be the next disclosure? Much more logical would have been to expand on the "Lord's" grievous anger.

Interestingly, and quite by accident, we found the passage that should have logically followed Gen. 6:7, but does not appear until the middle of the Bible. This chapter may have been "edited" to another part of the Bible because placed immediately after Gen. 6:7, too much would have been revealed about the reality of the hybrid creatures.

CHAPTER 7:

TRIAL & ERROR, EARLY RELIGIONS, & AN EXPERIMENT IN HUMAN PERCEPTION

O nce we understand that the involved extraterrestrial beings that genetically engineered *Homo sapiens* were not "gods," many things begin to make more sense. For instance, because they were not "gods" they did not know which religious doctrine or philosophy would be most effective in evolving humans spiritually. In fact, not only did they not know what religious doctrine would work best, but it appears that the entire idea that humans needed a religious doctrine seems to have caught the extraterrestrials flat footed. Initially, they had no plans for this aspect of human evolution. Zilch. Our evidence of this is that the first religions humans practiced seemed to have been based purely on fear of the unknown, or metaphysical applications, i.e., sorcery, magic, and witchcraft. No other philosophy or rhetoric seems to have been involved.

This leads us to a highly significant point in our UFO/ extraterrestrial investigation: That point being that the proof of the reality of extraterrestrials is evident as much in the mistakes and attempts to cover up these mistakes that they made, as it is in the sightings of UFOs, in the ancient civilizations they helped build, and in the technological advances they have given humans. It is a sort of left-handed or negative proof which may be a more revealing form of proof exactly because the extraterrestrials did not want to take credit for certain developments in human evolution.

In the vacuum of this psycho-spiritual over sight, the human psyche appears to have gravitated towards five main pseudo- religions: 1) Sorcery, magic, and witchcraft; 2) Ancestor worship; 3) Worship of some of the more powerful hybrid creatures as "gods"; 4) Worship of the giants mentioned in Genesis; and 5) Goddess worship.

Sorcery, Magic, and Witchcraft

Sorcery, magic and witchcraft may have been not so much religions or dogmas as much as simply remnants of the psychic abilities and fading intrinsic knowledge of the forces and principles of the universe that the early humans remembered from the former incarnations as hybrid creatures or from the pre-hybrid state of existence, as divine thoughts of the Creator. For instance, the ability and knowledge of how to project consciousness into another dimension, clothed in thought-energy, as another form, today, would be considered sorcery, magic, or witchcraft. Sorcery, magic and witchcraft would have been the first "technologies," and the abuse of the forces of the mind and the universe would have been the abuse of power that Edgar Cayce mentioned.

There are many rumors, that we could not confirm, that the ancient Sumerian texts contained many books (clay tablets) of magical incantations. These incantation were also mentioned in connection with the surgical and medical texts relative to healing. Another scrap of information that adds to the credence that magic and sorcery may have been the main religions of Sumer is that one of Enki's many titles was as the "God of Incantations."

There is also the unproven theory that the language that the ancient Sumerians spoke had the power to create, in a way that no language humans have spoken since had. It was a language that could manifest objects by "speaking" them.

The "gods," always studying and experimenting, may have given humans this language out of either pity or as a form of protection or to give humans a sense of divinity. The story of the "Tower of Babel," whereby human speech was "confounded," may represent the decision by the "gods" to recant this language of power. The early humans may have been creating folly with such power. The language was probably abused.[1]

Given the human propensity to abuse power, sorcery, magic, and witchcraft were probably actively suppressed by the extraterrestrials, after a brief experiment allowing humans to openly use it. (Biblically, witches were burned.)

Ancestor Worship

Ancestor worship would have spontaneously evolved from that ancient volatile period of great uncertainties and unknowns and the natural mystique surrounding the death of a loved one or an enemy. Possibly motivated by a deep primal fear of the dead, ancestor worship would have been a natural way to appease the dead, and keep them dead, by offering homage to them. Since the "gods" had offered nothing to replace or overcome this primal fear, this may be an indication that they, as yet, had no religious doctrines in place.

Worship of the Hybrid Creatures

Fear of the differences and superior abilities of some of the more powerful or more intelligent hybrid creatures would have rendered some of the hybrid creatures natural objects of worship, as well. Egyptian religion, statues, and wall or tomb paintings are full of depictions of "gods" with human bodies and animal heads.

Worship of the Giants

The worship of the giants, mentioned in Genesis, however, is an altogether different matter. Here we have a major blunder by the "gods." What could be called a "Prime Directive Distortion" of unprecedented magnitude. The cover-up of the worship of the giants was much more thorough than the Adam mistake. But, incredibly, as before, the extraterrestrials still left vital clues. Putting the pieces together, this is what appears to have happened:

The Anunnaki arrive on Earth, set up operations and begin to study the problem of the human souls trapped in thought-form dream-image projections.

144,000 earth years later, Ninhursag begins the ground breaking genetic experiments that will create the Adam. She is joined later in the experiments by her husband Enki. Together they fashion the Adam--The Model Man—The Prototype.

Adam behaves contrary to his design parameters and fornicates with the animals, the hybrid creatures, and the mutinying members of the Anunnaki [?], thumbing his nose at the extraterrestrials when they suggest he stop this behavior. These unpredicted sexual unions result in a sub-race of giants [the *Nephilim*].The creation of a sub-race of giants was never part of the extraterrestrial plan, and, in fact, represented a major deviation from what they had intended. It was an unforeseen genetic catastrophe of incalculable proportions.

Whoops.

Timeout: The offspring of the sexual union of the race of Adam with the mixtures is recorded in Genesis:

> "There were giants in the earth in those days; and also after that, when the sons of God [the race of Adam] came in unto the daughters of men [the mixtures], and they bare children to them, the same became mighty men which were of old, men of renown."[2] (Gen. 6:4)

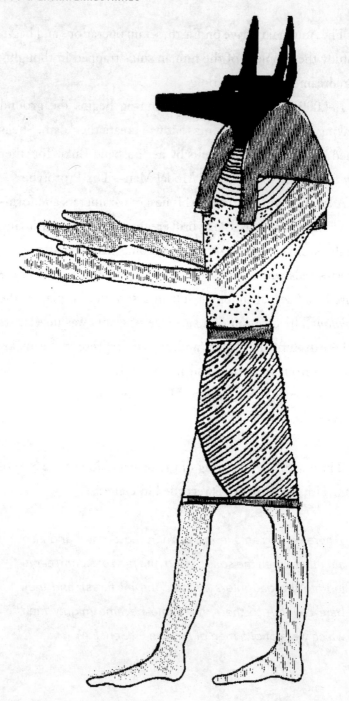

"Men of renown?" The Bible does not name these "mighty men which were of old, men of renown." But it's not hard to connect the dots, for the story of some of these giants, (these offspring of the sexual union of the "sons of God" with the "daughters of men") survived in the tales of what we think of as Greek "mythology." Some of them were "mythologically known as the "Titans." We all know who the "Titans" were. In *Edith Hamilton Mythology Timeless Tales of Gods and Heroes*, Edith Hamilton writes:

> The Titans, often called the Elder Gods, were for untold ages supreme in the universe. They were of enormous size and incredible strength. There were many of them, but only a few of them appeared in stories of mythology. The most important of which was Cronus..."
>
> -Edith Hamilton (*Mythology*- 1940)

The "Titans," also known as the "Twelve Great Olympians" were Zeus; Poseidon; Hades (also called Pluto); Hestia; Hera (Juno), Ares (Mars); Athena (Minerva), Apollo, Aphrodite (Venus); Hermes (Mercury); Artemis (Diana); and Hephaestus (Vulcan). Before Christianity, these were the "gods" of classic Greece and Rome!-:-"the mighty men which were of old, men of renown."

All of the giants weren't worshipped as "gods." Some were just royal pains in the neck. Professor Elaine Pagels, quoting *The Book of the Watchers*, says that some of these giants ate all the food of the people. When the people could no longer feed them, the giants ate the people.

Because they may have been shocked by these unpredicted turn of events, the extraterrestrials may have been temporarily paralyzed with uncertainty in regard to what to do next. They may also have finally glimpsed the interplanetary cultural dynamic (The "Prime Directive") whereby any outside intervention or attempt to help an alien culture will warp the fabric of that civilization in unforeseen ways.

If their actions in this situation were consistent with how they had behaved in the ancient texts, they took a couple of steps back and studied the frightening new development. That would explain why the giants survived as long as they did. If the Anunnaki were nothing else, they were patient and methodical. Let's not forget that 1 of their years (shar) still equalled 3,600 earth years. If they took several of their years to study the new development, 8,000, 9,000, 10,000 or more earth years might have past.

Logically, they would have studied the human psyche's religious tendencies and motivations, and its propensity to worship various external symbols of divinity, power or sources of fear; the dead ancestors, the hybrids, and the giants. They would have also contemplated what to do about the giants. Whether the giants were a good thing or a bad thing, and whether or not they could be manipulated or influenced to be surrogate "gods," may have been the topic of intense investigation by the extraterrestrials. These studies may also have prolonged their existence.

From the texts of Genesis 6, it is impossible to determine how much time elapsed from Gen 6:1, when the texts is stating the reality of the giants, to Gen 6:7, when the "Lord" is declaring that He will destroy them all. Regardless of the amount of time that elapsed, our guess is that in the interim, the extraterrestrials had thoroughly studied the problem of the giants, and arrived at the conclusion that the only solution was to destroy the giants, destroy the race of Adam, and destroy the mixtures. Then to begin again with a clean slate.

Whether or not the giants (the "Titans") were destroyed in the flood, or whether the Anunnaki hunted them down and murdered them is not clear. All we know for certain is that, except for the giant Goliath, the giants are not mentioned again in any biblical context.

After the giants, the race of the Adam and the hybrid creatures had been exterminated, the extraterrestrial's effort from these early periods onward may have been a combination of suppression of the old beliefs, as they cropped up, and experimentation with various religious philosophies and doctrines that could bring about true spiritual awakening in humans. Again, because they were not "gods," they did not know which form of religious doctrine would be most effective.

Goddess Worship

After or perhaps during the practices of sorcery, magic, and witchcraft, the worship of the giants, the worship of the hybrid creatures, and ancestor worship, the first major, positive religion (i.e., a religion not based solely on fear or terror of some unknown force or entity) seems to have been Goddess worship. In humanity's infancy, a loving mother symbol of divinity would have been much more comforting than the stern, impersonal male deities that became predominate later. It would make perfect sense if early humans found comfort in worshipping a female—Mother Goddess-- concept of a Supreme Deity.

Besides the naturally comforting aspect of a Mother Goddess, a contributing factor was that primitive people, initially, did not associate the sex act with having children. They believed that women "miraculously" had children.[4] That women could bring forth life and men could not create a positive mystique about women and a female goddess.

A positive aspect of Goddess worship, from the perspective of the extraterrestrials, was that Goddess worship glorified several of the Anunnaki women. In *When God Was A Woman*, by Merlin Stone (1976), Merlin Stone was convinced that all the names she had uncovered, in her research of Goddess worship were different names for the same Goddess. Her list of Goddess' names, however, may actually represent many different Anunnaki (extraterrestrial) women. She names "Innin, Inanna, Nana, Nut, Anahita, Ishtar, Isis, Au Set, Ishara, Asherah, Ashtart, Attoret, Attarand Hathor— the many named Divine Ancestress." We know from Zecharia Sitchin's *The 12th Planet* that Isis and Inanna were not the same woman.

Another positive aspect of Goddess worship was that it may have been the first major religion that was based as much on love or gratitude for what the Mother Goddess had given humans, as on fear.

Merlin Stone, in *When God Was A Woman* (1976), places the rein of Goddess worship from about 9,000 to 7,000 BC. to 500AD.

"In every area of the Near and Middle East the Goddess was known in historic times. Though many centuries of transformation had undoubtedly changed the religion in various ways, the worship of the female deity survived into the classical periods of Greece and Rome. It was not totally suppressed until the time of the Christian emperors of Rome and Byzantium, who closed down the last Goddess temples in about 500 AD."

-Merlin Stone
(When God Was A Woman-1976)

Despite the positivity of Goddess worship, that it cultivated love and gratitude in humans for a supreme being, and despite the fact that it glorified several Anunnaki females, some aspect of Goddess worship deeply disturbed the "gods," and the extraterrestrials began an active campaign to suppress and destroy it starting at about 7,000 BC. (*When God Was A Woman*)

Trial and Error

At the same time sorcery, magic, witchcraft and Goddess worship were being suppressed or annihilated, the extraterrestrials began introducing slightly different religious doctrines and disciplines into different cultures and among different ethnic peoples. To the Semitic peoples (the Jews) they gave the

85

Kabalah, they also gave a Gnostic (direct knowing) approach to spirituality (see *The Nag Hammadi Library*). They gave the fundamental principles of Christianity, in the tenants of the Hebrew form of worship.

In the East, Yoga, Zen, and The Vedic texts were "received" from the "gods." According to Islam, "God" gave Mohammed the Koran. Once these religious doctrines · had been in place, they then simply stood back and observed which doctrine produced the most masters, or the most devout worshippers.

Our point of this brief synopsis of the early religions is to attempt to present a composite sketch of the evolution and development of humans relative to extraterrestrial influences (or non-influences), as well as to demonstrate that the pattern of extraterrestrial intervention in human civilizations and evolution that has not involved giving humans technology or building civilizations has consistently been one of experimentation, or simply watching and observing before deciding to suppress a doctrine or philosophy, or introduce one. Trying different approaches to see what works best, because past experiences had made it quite clear that human behavior was, at times, totally unpredictable. Indications are that this experimental approach was deemed the safest way to proceed.

The Adam Experiment

The revelation that the race of Adam were androgynous creatures may be another example of the extraterrestrial's need to experiment and run tests on humans to calibrate or ascertain human responses. What do humans deduce from what stimuli?

What most effectively motivates or influences human perceptions and behavior? What subtle or subliminal words or images most quickly triggers recognition in both the conscious and subconscious mind? Which clues are more effective?

Since they did not know, and past failures had convinced them of human unpredictability, they logically would have tried different approaches in an attempt to better understand human responses.

The revelation that Adam was an androgynous creature may have been such an experiment in human perception.

In Genesis, the primary clue that the race of the Adam were androgynous creatures was a single unclear reference contained in the line that ended: " ...male and female created he them." From that reference we are left with mostly uncertainty. Maybe they were created as male and female in a single being, maybe they weren't. Only by correlating that fragment of information with other less cryptic sources (i.e., Cayce, Plato, Blavatsky and the *Kabalah*) can we conclude that the race of the Adam were androgynous.

In Genesis, we are given only this literary clue—just words. In the East, in Indian religious texts, we are given graphics, pictorial representations of the deities Sri Krishna and Shiva, Lord of the Dance, just to name a couple. Without a single word of explanation, these elaborate and colorful paintings show these "demi-gods" as having four arms. In the *Bhagavad Gita*, the texts says that Krishna's true form is "four armed." That's it. No other explanation of why Krishna has four arms is forth coming. Apparently, he just does. End of mystery.

Since I had read some of the *Bhagavad Gita* in the '70s, I had been aware of these four armed paintings of Krishna and Shiva for several decades. Though in all honesty, I had never known quite what to make of them. Not sure of what, if anything, would become clearer this time, I reexamined these paintings, just out of curiosity.

Immediately, I remembered an old confusion I'd had about the pictures of Krishna. Krishna is constantly referred to in masculine terms, i.e., "Lord Krishna." He is the best friend of a warrior prince named Arjuna. They are depicted both in pictures and in the *Bhagavad Gita* texts as best buddies. Arjuna respects Krishna's advice as one would respect the advice of an older and wiser brother, whom one deeply loves. There is not the slightest hint that their friendship is in any way sexual or inappropriate. Yet, Krishna has got to be the most beautiful male you have ever seen.

Initially, I had attributed this to the fact that the ancient artists wanted to show divinity as great physical beauty. Krishna was a demi-god and, therefore, extremely beautiful. But as I gazed at the picture, that explanation no longer seemed to fit. His features are soft, delicate. He wears elegant and elaborate pearl necklaces; long gold hooped earrings, a golden crown, flowing feminine robes. Krishna appears to be wearing a blue powder makeup, black eyeliner, and ruby red lipstick. His hair is long and flowing and jet black. Yet, he is always depicted as bare chested. Showing the unmistakable chest of a male. (See sketch)

In these elaborate colorful paintings, next to the other harder looking males, Krishna looks like a very sexually desirable woman, four arms or no. The old confusion was that I never understood why Krishna, a demi-god, was always represented as so beautiful and delicate.

It is a basic psychology of religion that a "god" should look like His or Her people. If not, then, the people will not sufficiently identify with Him or Her being their god. Then it dawned, Krishna was a graphic, though perhaps mostly symbolic, representation of the first humans (after the hybrids)-- Four armed and androgynous--a true hermaphrodite having both a penis and a vagina, with, however, *predominately feminine features*. Lord Krishna was an ancient artist's rendition of one of the "sons of God," the race of the Adam. At one time, Krishna must have looked like His or/Her people. Otherwise, a four armed "god" makes no sense,i.e., would not be recognized by the people as "their" "god." This religious psychological axiom would have been more prevalent in antiquity than it would be today. And it is still of consequence today, as can be exhibited by the fact that Christ is always depicted as being white--Caucasian. This allows whites to identify with Christ. While blacks believe that God, Allah, is black. Which allows blacks to identify with their God. To the Indians, God is depicted as being Indian, and so on.

Subconsciously, I had assumed (as I am sure the "gods" intended) that the "race of Adam" (Adam being a somewhat masculine name), also known as "the sons of God" ("sons" is distinctly masculine) would have masculine features. But where is it written that an androgynous being--a true hermaphrodite--will have masculine features? It's not written anywhere. The genetically engineered race of Adam were genetically engineered to be sexually self-desiring, sexually self-reproducing hermaphrodites, with a penis and a vagina and predominately beautiful feminine features. Krishna is an androgynous being is what the colorful, elaborate paintings implied.

As if perception had been the missing key all along, the symbolic objects Krishna is holding in each of his four hands suddenly became predominate in the painting of Krishna. Krishna's forward most left hand holds a very big club--a phallic symbol if you ever saw one. Krishna's farthest away left hand holds a conch shell. I do not know what the conch shell is supposed to symbolize, but it looks like a vagina--a feminine symbol. That Krishna is holding both a club and the conch shell--male and female symbols--would lead us to believe that the artist is trying to tell us that Krishna is himself or herself both male and female in one being. The symbolism in the elaborate painting screams this.

That a four armed creature could appear so beautiful was also something I had never before considered. I had also assumed that an androgynous creature would be hideous in appearance. That the genetic scientists Enki and Ninhursag would have made them beautiful was something I had never considered.

Jumping Ship

If the "sons of God" (the race of Adam) were, indeed, a race of hermaphrodites with predominately beautiful feminine features, that would also explain why in both Zecharia Sitchin's translation and in Professor Elaine Pagels' research in *The Book of the Watcher's* the Anunnaki flight crew were willing to mutiny. The texts say that they "lusted after 'human' women." If the race of Adam, the "sons of God" all look like males, then, why would a bunch of extraterrestrial men (the texts say 200) want them badly enough to risk the wrath of a flight commander who had a temper and the technological weaponry and expertise to annihilate the entire planet? If the race of Adam all looked like men, then, that scenario doesn't make sense. But if Ninhursag and Enki genetically engineered the "sons of God" (the race of Adam) to look like beautiful sexually desirable women, then it fits. The mutiny now makes sense.

The Anunnaki flight crew members were willing to mutiny and to pay with their lives to have sexual intercourse with these creatures--these "human" women. A price, according to Genesis, they, indeed, paid.

The Suppression of Goddess Worship

Another riddle that is partially solved, if the "sons of God" all looked like beautiful women, was the destruction of cultures and people who were Goddess worshippers.

There was a very dark and troublesome transitional period in the evolution of religious beliefs of the human species. Initially, Goddess worship was as respected as God worship among ancient peoples. Then about 7,000 years ago, a campaign was launched to eliminate the temples, shrines, and the people who worshipped the Goddess. There were horrible massacres and blood baths that are recorded in the Bible. These massacres were ordered by "God."--Yahweh-- the male deity. Women, children and old people were all ruthlessly killed to stamp out and repress Goddess worship.

The suppression of Goddess worship by wholesale, cold-blooded murder of children, old people, and women was deeply disturbing. Since these murders were ordered by Yahweh, it was doubly so. Goddess worshippers were apparently doing something that royally ticked off the "gods." (We will examine this reason in more detail in "Part II. The Genesis Conspiracy.")

Our point is, did the hermaphrodites appearance as women influence the "gods" behavior in ways we would never have dreamed possible?

CHAPTER 8:

TOUGH LOVE:"THE LINES OF CONFUSION"
THE ALIEN'S SOLUTION TO THE MIXTURES

> *"Wildcats shall meet with hyenas, goat-demons shall call to each other; there too Lilith shall repose, and find a place to rest.*
> *There shall the owl nest and lay and hatch and brood in its shadow."*
>
> *-Isaiah 34:14*

Remember Genesis 6:1 and 6:2? *"And it came to pass, when men began to multiply on the face of the earth, and daughters were born unto them.*

2. That the sons of God saw the daughters of men that they were fair; and took them wives of all which they chose."

"Daughters of men" is left undefined. It is impossible to tell from the above texts what the "daughters of men" looked like. Cayce said that "daughters of men" was a coded reference to the mixtures- the hybrid creatures.

It is no accident that Genesis never gives a description of the "daughters of men." Realize that Genesis was not arbitrarily edited. It was not edited for clarity, or to be made more comprehensible to the masses. The editors of Genesis had a particular theme or point of view they were trying to create. Relative to this theme, it was important that it *not* be realized who or what the "daughters of men" were, and that they were real.

Yet, true to form, the extraterrestrials seemed reluctant to completely destroy so vital a clue to humankind's pre-historic past. Instead of encrypting or encoding it, they left this reference as is, then simply hid it. They moved it from Genesis 7, where it logically belongs, to Isaiah 34. Few people have ever heard of Isaiah 34. Fewer people still have actually read it because it's practically in the middle of the Bible. We only found it by accident. We were trying to verify another piece of information given in a Cayce reading, whereby Cayce said that the first human consciousness to materialize in three-dimensional earth reality was the very first female (even before Eve) named Lilith.

Cayce's casual mention of Lilith was another vital clue. If Lilith was real, then she is the keystone in the entire UFO-extraterrestrial-human origin puzzle. The proof of her reality would be proof of the first cause of human existence, or proof of the first step in a sequence of events that has led to the entirety of human history and human evolution, and the need for extraterrestrial intervention. She, not Eve, would be the true mother of the human species, not in its present form, but the reason for the necessity of the present form. If other unrelated sources also made mention of her, in ways that indicated her reality, it would be the subtlest of proofs of the existence of UFOs and extraterrestrials because it would simultaneously validate the reality of the mixtures (for she was the first "mixture," the first "daughter of men"), entrapment, and the need for a "rescue mission."

The flesh and blood reality of Lilith was the key to it all, so we looked for traces of her actual existence everywhere we could think.

As it turned out, the mentions of Lilith are not confined to the Cayce readings. Besides the Cayce mention of Lilith, The "Tattered Cover" bookstore, in Denver, had a book on Lilith, a collection of stories called *Lilith's Cave Jewish Tales of the Supernatural Selected And Retold* by Howard Schwartz (Oxford University Press--1988).

Zecharia Sitchin also mentions Lilith in his translations of the ancient Sumerian texts. In *The Wars of Gods and Men*, Mr. Sitchin says:

"The conspiracy of Zu and his evil plotting remained also in mankind's memory, evolving into a fear of birdlike demons who can cause affliction and pestilence. Some of these demons were called *Lillu,* a term that played on the double meaning "to howl" and "of the night"; their female leader, Lillitu-- Lilith--was depicted as a naked, winged goddess with birdlike feet. The many *shurpu* ("purification by burning") texts that have . been found were formulas for incantations against these evil spirits-- forerunners of the sorcery and witchcraft that had lasted throughout the millennia."

-Zecharia Sitchin
(The Wars of Gods and Men - 1985)

In *Lilith's Cave Jewish Tales of the Supernatural*, there are 40 stories many of which make mention of this first pre-human, hybrid creature. The rite of circumcision is closely associated with her, as are amulets bearing the names of three "angels" sent to retrieve her: *Senay, Sansenoy,* and *Semangelof*

Of course, none of this is concrete proof of Lilith's actual existence, but it is impressive circumstantial evidence: Why the myriad of stories and legends about Lilith unless, at some point, there was a physical, real life basis for those stories that have survived for millenniums?

While searching the Internet for any and all references to Lilith, there was a mention of Lilith that said its source was the Bible. It was a short verse that read:

"Wildcats shall meet with hyenas; goat-demons[1] shall call to each other; there too Lilith shall repose, and find a place to rest; There shall the owl nest and lay and hatch and brood in its shadow."

-Isaiah 34:14

When I turned to Isaiah 34:14 to verify the quote, I was disappointed to see that "Lilith" had been translated "owl" in the King James version of the Bible. Perhaps the translator(s) of the Bible thought that "owl" would have more meaning than "Lilith" to a more modern constituency, or perhaps they sought to dispel any and all superstitions connected to the old beliefs.

It is very easy for a translation to be inaccurate or a misinterpretation due to the ambiguous nature of certain words or concepts, or because some words are not translatable: The King James version said "owl," logic and instinct suggested that "Lilith" was the original concept meant here--the "Eve" of the monstrosities.

To test the theory that the King James reference to "owl," in Isaiah 34, really referred to "Lilith" and not to an ordinary hoot owl, we read the entire biblical chapter. Reading the entire chapter, "hoot owl" didn't fit. "Lilith" fit. "Lilith" fit because ALL of the creatures mentioned in this biblical chapter were either hybrid beings right out of the legends and mythology, or they were the types of animals the earthbound pre-Adam souls were famous for incarnating as. That's why "Lilith" fit.

Here were the descriptive names of the creatures that were called the "daughters of men" were, and they were conspicuously missing from Genesis 6. Had this chapter remained in Genesis, any one who read the first books of the Bible could have deduced the truth--that is, who and what the "daughters of men"

The Isaiah chapter speaks directly to or of the *unicorn, Lilith* [the Great Owl], *dragons, satyrs*, goats, rams, bulls, and two types of birds *(cormorant:* a large black sea bird; *bittern:* a marsh bird related to the heron) that may or may not have been mixtures (our guess is that they were). The fact that all of the creatures mentioned in this biblical chapter were right out of legends or the types of animals the pre-Adam souls liked to incarnate as, raised an eyebrow. The "Lord's" (alien/"gods"?) reaction to them raised both. For here is apparently what the aliens had decided to do about the mixtures.[2] The alien solution was not necessarily created out of malice, but it was obviously committed with "divine" wrath and righteous indignation. The decision that the "council of the gods" may have reached was that the only way to permanently "free" the mixtures from multiple cycles of incarnations as hybrid creatures was to make those hybrid bodies *unavailable*, i.e., to kill them all! Genocide. That way they (the souls who had incarnated as mixtures) were forced to return in the bodies of the new humans—the Adama--the "safe vessel."

In its heavily symbolic language, this is precisely what the Bible *seems* to be saying the "Lord" (alien/"gods) did to the mixtures. (Note: The numbers do not correspond to the actual biblical passages:)

1. *For the indignation of the Lord is upon all nations, and his fury upon all their armies* [Why? What had ALL nations done?]: *he hath utterly destroyed them, he hath delivered them to the slaughter...*

2. *For my sword shall be bathed in heaven:* [possible interpretation: "I/we are going to destroy you because it's the right thing to do"?] *behold, it shall come down upon I-du-me a, and upon the people of my curse, to judgment.*

3. *The sword of the Lord is filled with blood, it is made fat with fatness* [possible interpretation: "heavy with gore"?], *and with the blood of lambs and goats, with the fat of kidneys of rams: for the Lord hath a sacrifice in Bozrah, and a great slaughter in the land of I-du-me a.*

4. *And the* **unicorns** *shall come down with them, and the bullocks with the bulls; and their land shall be soaked*

with blood, and their dust made fat with fatness.

5. *For it is the day of the Lord's vengeance, and the year of recompenses* [to repay or reward] *for the controversy of Zion.* [Were the mixtures the "controversy of Zion?"]

6. *But the cormorant and the bittern shall possess it; and he shall stretch out upon it* **the lines of confusion**, *and the stones of emptiness*[3]

7. *And thorns shall come up in her palaces, nettles and brambles in the fortresses*[4] *thereof and it shall be an habitation of dragons, and a court of owls* [Lilith].

8. *The wild beast of the desert shall also meet with the wild beast of the island, and the* **satyr** *shall cry to his fellow; the screech owl* [Lilith] *also shall rest there, and find for herself a place of rest.*

9. *There shall the great owl* [Lilith] *make her nest, and lay, and hatch, and gather under her shadow: there shall the vultures also be gathered, every one with her mate.*

10. *Seek ye out of the book of the Lord, and read: no one of these shall fail, none shall want her mate: for my mouth it hath commanded, and his spirit it hath gathered them.*

11. *And he hath cast the lot for them, and his hand hath divided it unto them by line: they shall possess it for ever, from generation to generation shall they dwell therein.*

An interesting phenomenon, that we have not had an opportunity to comment on before, concerning the extraterrestrial use of human languages, is a very distinguishing linguistic trait that seemed to pepper any quotations taken directly from the "gods." You could almost call it an accent, or a linguistic "signature." Whether it was because of their love of words or their love of multi-dimensional meanings or whether they did it to demonstrate that perception was the key--that the same idea or word perceived from another level of understanding changed (or added to) its meaning entirely. The extraterrestrials loved words with multiply meanings. They loved metaphor and symbolism. The creation myth is full of words with double and triple meanings. For example, man is called a "lulu," a primitive worker. The initial meaning seems to be that man was created to work for the "gods." But from another level, primitive worker could also mean one who must work off a karmic debt or obligation, in a primitive way.

Our second observation concerning Isaiah 34, is that the entire chapter is written in this linguistic "signature of the gods"-- heavy metaphor or multiple play on word meanings--which suggest that the prophet Isaiah may have taken dictation directly from the "gods," or the "god's" messengers for this chapter. That is, he may have rendered it exactly as the "Lord", or a "messenger of the Lord"—a lieutenant or an air man of low rank among the flight crew of the Anunnaki-- dictated it to him.

The last paragraph seems to read that the "Lord" decided their fate, *"cast the lot for them,"* based on their genealogy--*"by line."*

The other subtle reference to what seems to be the heart of this chapter seems to be, *"But the cormorant and the bittern* (large sea birds) *shall possess it: and he shall stretch out upon it the lines of confusion."* The *"lines of confusion"* is an obvious reference to the hybrids, the mixtures [5.]

Whether or not the aliens exterminated the mixtures this biblical chapter would indicate that they were aware and displeased with them.

In all honesty, I am not entirely sure what the aliens did. Some passages of the Bible might as well have been written in ancient Greek, as far as my ability to decipher them is concerned. Whether the mixtures were quarantined or killed is not completely clear. The first part of the Isaiah 34 chapter suggests that they were slaughtered. The last part of the Isaiah 34 chapter suggests that they were put in some terrible place where they would stay "from generation to generation shall they dwell there in."

My guess is that the aliens declared war on the mixtures, corralled them into some terrible place, and eventually, perhaps, methodically, killed them all--so that the trapped souls would be "free" from the prison of endless cycles of existence as mixtures. And since the Anunnaki believed that the binding force that initially entrapped them was carnal nature, sexual morality was one of the first lessons the aliens would try to teach the new humans--with only marginal success.

Finally, whether the mixtures were butchered or quarantined, this biblical reference adds weight to the circumstantial evidence of their actual existence. It also validates Cayce's claim that the "daughters of men" were the hybrid creatures believed for millenniums to be only mythology. For in the linguistic, poetic signature of the "gods," the Anunnaki called them "the lines of confusion."

Bull with human head cylinder seal clay impression. This is a sketch of a photo found in the book *The Emergence of Man The First Cities*, by Dora Jane Hamblin.1973.A Time-LifeBook.

Bird with human head. This sketch is from *Chapters of the Coming Forth by Day* papyrus-Ninteenth Dynasty - Egypt. Found in the book *The Pyramids and the Sphinx*, by Desmond Stewart. 1979. A Newsweek Book.

CHAPTER 9:

THE FOUNDER OF BABYLON, OANNES THE MUSARUS ANNEDOTUS

> *"We may discover that the ancient world, the further one goes back in time, tends to develop a more and more odd flavor. The mysteries become denser, the strangeness thicker and more viscous."*
>
> -Robert K.G. Temple
>
> *(The Sirius-Mystery)*

The Lines of Confusion

We have tried to prove the reality of UFOs and extra-terrestrials not by validating UFO sightings or photographs, not by validating alien abduction stories, or that back-engineered technologies exist. Our proof has not involved UFO conspiracy theories, or that our military or government struck a deal with the Grays. We have tried to prove the existence of UFOs and extraterrestrials by focusing on the possible root cause of their presence: The "rescue" of the hybrid creatures mentioned in the Cayce readings.

In Isaiah 34, these *pre-Adam* humans were metaphorically called *"the lines of confusion."* These were the unicorns, the dragons, the satyrs, the bulls, the Great Owl, the hybrid creatures that for millenniums have been believed to be only mythology. We have tried to scientifically prove that the Genesis reference to the "daughters of men" was yet another biblical code name for this ancient bizarre entrapment of human consciousness, and that this folly was the heart of the dark secret of humanity's Earthly origins.

We have also tried to prove that the creation of Adam and Eve, in the Garden of Eden, represented a genetic attempt by the extraterrestrials (known as the Anunnaki) at a solution to this bizarre problem. That Adam and Eve do NOT represent humanity's first habitation in this dimension. This was also cryptically hinted at in the Cayce readings.

We know it is difficult for the modern rational mind to accept the idea that we were ever anything other than what we are—what we seem to be—entirely human. The very idea that we were ever in any other body type seems ludicrous, at best, the stuff of bad science fiction or science fantasy.

And yet, there is an inescapable logic here, as exact and precise as the solution to an algebraic equation. If we insert this single idea—that Edgar Cayce spoke the truth, that the first humans were not Adam and Eve, but the "daughters of men" (Lilith and the myriad of thought-form projected hybrid creatures), and that the "God" of Genesis is actually the Anunnaki scientists Ninhursag, Enki, and the Anunnaki high command –if we insert this single idea into the mysterious equation of humanity's origin and evolution and the likelihood of extraterrestrial intervention in those origins and evolution, the known scientific evolutionary anomalies and mysteries start to immediately make a lot more sense. The puzzle pieces start to immediately smoothly fit together.

This single idea would explain why we cannot completely trace our evolution from apes; it would explain the fully modern anatomy of *Australopethicus Africanus* (the south African ape); it would explain Cro-Magon's sudden, otherwise, inexplicable culture and intelligence; it would explain the ancient "sudden civilization" of Sumer that seemed to spring up full blown out of nowhere, overnight; it would explain the Sumerian, Assyrian, Babylonian, Egyptian, Roman, and Greek artistic fascination with painting, sculpturing, and putting on carved stone cylinder seals bizarre creatures like the Sphinx, Pan, centaurs, bulls with human heads, humans with bird heads, birds with human heads, and griffins; it would explain Isaiah 34 and why the Bible is talking about unicorns, satyrs, dragons, bulls, and the Great Owl (Lilith); it would explain why every ancient culture has a mythology about hybrid creatures; it would explain who the God in Genesis is talking to when he says, "Let us make man in our image; after our likeness;" it would explain why sexual intercourse with an animal was a capital offense among the ancient Jews; it would explain why the animal was also put to death in such sexual unions (out of the fear that some hideous hybrid creature might have been conceived during that illicit sexual union); it would explain why the Anunnaki lied in the *Enuma elish*, and what they were trying to conceal.

Press this one piece into our evolutionary puzzle and everything else immediately starts to make a lot more sense.

Still, we know it is a lot to accept. No matter how convincing the evidence or how reliable the sources of that evidence or how many questions this solution seems to answer. The idea that humans once existed as these ancient monstrosities boggles the imagination and is automatically rejected out of hand as too fantastic, too impossible to be real.

With this understandable skepticism in mind, we would like to present a couple of more pieces of hard physical evidence that we hope will further substantiate our premise. These additional pieces of hard physical evidence can be found in the deeper understanding of exactly who founded the ancient civilization of Babylon, in the linguistic clues hidden in the word "Babylon," and in re-examining the depictions the ancient people left us of these pre-Adam humans (and those pre-Adam humans who were still in hybrid creature form after the race of Adam had been genetically created).

Who Founded Babylon?

Babylon is famous for two of the seven wonders of the ancient world; The Hanging Gardens of Babylon, and its great wall (both were breathtaking architectural achievements); famous for its sixth king Hammurabi, "The Law Giver" (1792-1750 B.C.) and what was once believed to be the very first codes of laws for civilized humans; famous for Nebuchadnezzar (604-562 B.C.), of biblical fame, who caputed Jerusalem in 586 B.C.[1] and exiled many of the Jews to Babylon; and who built the Hanging Gardens of Babylon for his wife, Amytis, the daughter of the King of Medes, who missed her forest homelands.[2]

As can be seen from just these few examples of its surviving history, Babylon was a thriving, cultured, highly sophisticated and advanced civilization. It had conquered Sumer and Jerusalem. "It was known to the ancient Greeks and Romans as the greatest city-state of its time."[3] It was, in fact, "the cultural and economic center of the ancient world for 600 years."[4] In its prime, it was the ancient equivalent of an America in its cultural and economic superiority and as a world power.

Yet, despite Babylon's greatness and the artifacts and records that have survived, little is known of how that ancient civilization actually came into being. The accepted theory of how Babylon came into existence doesn't quite answer the question of Babylon's fame and legendary achievements, though it does answer the question of how that great ancient first civilization, Sumer, fell.

Babylon, the Accepted Theory of Its Origin

The British novelist and author of several non-fiction books on ancient Mesopotamia, James Wellard, relates the accepted archaeological theory on Babylon's origins in his book *Babylon A History of the Greatest City of the Ancient World and Its Rediscovery by Modern Archaeologists* (1972):

"It was one of those periodic migrations [of entire nations or federations of tribes] around 2500 B.C. that threatened the very existence of the Sumerian city-states. The invaders seem to have come out of south Arabia, though all we know about them was that they were called the

Amurru by the Sumerians and were probably the same people the Hebrews refer to as Amorites or Canaanites. The Bible describes the latter people as giants whom the Israelites found in occupation of Palestine on their arrival in that country.

Who ever the Amurru were, or by whatever name they were called, they swarmed into the Mesopotamian plains, captured the towns, killed the local kings, and then settled down to enjoy the advantages of civilized life. It was these people who were to create the Babylonian state whose first chieftain king appears on the stage of history in about 2300 B.C. His name was Sargon L..not to be confused with Sargon II of Assyria (721-705 B.C.).[p.111]

-James Wellard
(Babylon A History of the Greatest
City of the Ancient World ..- 1972)

The accepted archaeological understanding of how Babylon came into existence was that it was the result of the conquest of Sumer, in 2500 B.C., when a "federation of tribes of barbarian nomads suddenly burst out of the deserts of Arabia or descended from the steppes of Asia and swarmed on· to the settled agricultural communities of Mesopotamia"[5] (i.e., Sumer). These Bronze Age barbarians called the Amurru by the Sumerians (also possibly known as the Canaanites, or Amorites) set up a police state until around 2303 B.C., when Sargon I took power marking the beginning of the First Dynasty.

James Wellard describes the conquering nomadic horde as "Bronze Age barbarians." He implies that the Sumerians were conquered by a more savage, though less cultured and less technologically advanced people. The cultural and technological *inferiority* of the conquering Amurru is the major inconsistency or flaw with the theory that the conquest of Sumer was the beginning of the advanced Babylon civilization.

By this we mean Sargon I created a dynasty that lasted from 2303 to 2108B.C., or about 200 years. Before Sargon I, the Amurru had ruled Babylon from 2500B.C. to 2300 B.C. That's another 200 years. So, after almost 400 years of domination by the Amurru/Canaanite barbarians (twice the amount of time the United States has been in existence), there is no hint of the great teeming civilization that was to become Babylon.

Mr. Wellard makes the observation that at the end of this 400 years of domination that, "As yet this empire was not the centralized autocracy which was later to be characteristic of Babylonian, Assyrian, and Persian empires, but was still a loose confederation of allied city-states kept loyal to the most powerful of the kings by a large standing army." i.e., It was *still* a police state after nearly 400 years of domination! No Hanging Gardens. No distinctive culture or economy. Just conquered Mesopotamian territories that were in a constant state of rebellion.

Our point is that *the conquering of Sumer, in 2500 B.C., was not the beginning of the famous Babylon civilization.* If the Amurru/Canaanites were truly the source of Babylon's eventual great cultural and economic advances, there were no signs of it during those first 400 years, after conquest.

Further evidence that the first 400 years that the Amurru/ Canaanites ruled the conquered Sumerian city-states was not the cultural beginning of Babylon can be found in the book called simply *Babylon* (1996), by Joan Oates.

In Joan Oates' book *Babylon*, Ms. Oates points out that the conquered Mesopotamian territories were not called "Babylon" for some time:

> "As a geographical term Babylonia refers to the southern portion of the modern country of Iraq, ancient Mesopotamia, encompassing the land roughly between Baghdad at its northern limit and the head of the Arabian Gulf [to the south]. Historically, the term Babylonia reflects a relatively late unification of the country under Babylon's First Dynasty early in the 2nd millennium, though the word itself is of even later origin. From very early times the northern part of this land was referred to as Akkad and the southern as Sumer."[p.11]
>
> -Joan Oates
> *(Babylon - 1996)*

As Joan Oates points out, the name "Babylon" *"is of even later origin"* (than the First Dynasty in the 2nd millennium). That is, when Sumer was conquered and for at least 400 years after conquest, these conquered Sumerian city-states or territories where not yet even called Babylon. They were still known by their pre-occupation names of Akkad to the north and the many farming city-states of Sumer to the south. Though all of the forces and players seemed to be in place, there was technically still no Babylon. What was missing?

The question remains, then, that if the Amurru/Canaanite conquerors were not the source of Babylon's greatness, who or what was? And how does this answer further substantiate our premise that the "daughters of *men*"--"*the lines of confusion*"—were real?

That answer was found quite by accident in the book *The Sirius Mystery*, by Robert K.G. Temple (1976).

The Sirius Mystery

The Sirius Mystery, by Robert K.G. Temple, is the investigation of a tribe in Africa called the Dogan. The mystery Mr. Temple spent seven years investigating was how has a primitive tribe in Africa known for 5,000 years, and have as its central ideas of worship, precise astronomical understanding about the star system called Sirius?

For instance, their high priest believe that a star, which our scientists have only recently discovered and which cannot be seen with the naked eye called Sirius B, is the smallest, yet the heaviest star in the universe, and that the universe was born from this tiny white dwarf star[6]• Our scientists have discovered that Sirius B (known as "Digitaria" to the Dogan) is, indeed, a very dense white dwarf star which may be the heaviest star in the universe, though as to whether or not it gave "birth" to the universe cannot yet be validated.

The primitive Dagon tribal priests have known for 5,000 years that this invisible white dwarf star's orbit around Sirius A takes fifty years. They have known that the path of orbiting stars or planets is elliptical, not circular. That the Sirius star system is a binary (twin) star system, and that there are two foci, or two centers, not one. The Dogan priests are a virtual encyclopedia of information on the Sirius star system. Yet, in every other way, they remain a primitive African people.

How have a primitive African tribe known for 5,000 years what modern astronomers have only recently discovered? Is the focus of the Sirius Mystery. To make a long and complicated story short, the Dagon say that the "Nommos" instructed them. The "Nommos," according to Robert Temple's understanding, are extraterrestrials from the Sirius star system, amphibians who look more like fish or dolphins than anything else. They certainly don't look human.

As Mr. Temple tries to determine if any other ancient people might have passed this information on to the Dagon, he uncovered a very interesting body of information on ancient Egypt, Sumer, Babylon, and what the ancient people knew of the Sirius star system. Some of this information touched directly on his subject of the Dogan mystery. Some of it was only partially related. One of the interesting pieces of information he reveals are fragments from the writings of a Babylonian priest name Berossus. Berossus was writing a history of Babylon.

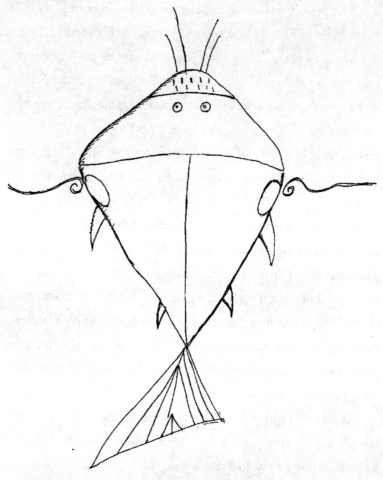

This is a sketch of the drawing the Dogon priest made of Nommo.

It is Berossus who reveals the true founders of Babylon and the source of Babylon's greatness.

In Appendix II of *The Sirius Mystery* are the fragments of the origin of the Babylonian culture as told by the Babylonian priest Berossus to the Greek historian Apollodorus:

"This is the history which Berossus has transmitted to us. He tells us that the first king was Alorus of Babylon, a Chaldaean; he reigned ten sari: and afterwards Alaparus, and Amelon who came from Pantibiblon: the Ammenon the Chaldaean, in whose time appeared the Musarus Oannes the Annedotus from the Erythraean sea (the Red Sea, the Persian Gulf, and the Indian Ocean, as known collectively in ancient times)."[p.248]

- Robert K.G. Temple

(*The Sirius Mystery*- 1976)

The Musarus Annedotus

The sentence fragment that concerns us and that has a direct bearing on our major premise is:" *in whose time appeared the Musarus Oannes the Annedotus from the Erythean sea.*"

Robert Temple, like any good researcher, was concerned that he did not know the meaning of the words "Musarus" and "Annedotus." When he discovered the meanings, he was shocked, not because of the complexity of the meanings, but because of their simplicity. His surprise was at the unnecessary use of words that would only tend to obscure the meanings instead of making them clear. Why use a couple of big unclear words when the words themselves would do? Perhaps it was out of politeness and gratitude to whoever this Oannes was? Perhaps it was out of embarrassment.

Whatever the reason, Robert Temple simply looked up the meanings and discovered that the meaning of "Musarus" is **"an abomination."** And the meaning of "Annedotus" is **"a repulsive one!"**--So, the phrase *"the Musarus Oannes the Annedotus"* meant that Oannes was a "repulsive abomination."

Linguistics and human nature are our keys to the authenticity of those two words. In that, the words "Musarus" and "Annedotus" were obviously a polite way of describing the creature Oannes. Why be diplomatically polite unless to use the actual descriptive words cause repercussions? Unless the use of the actual descriptive words be read by the "Musarus" "Annedotus" and he be offended. Why distinguish between a repulsive and a beautiful abomination unless there were actually beautiful and repulsive abominations?

From the Berossus fragments and the Dogon priests' drawings, Robert Temple already knew that Oannes was an amphibian, part fish and part man. However, Oannes was not easy to look at. His entire body was that of a large fish, but beneath the fish head was a human head, and coming from the fishtail, human legs. So that Oannes, from the drawings, appears to be a human man inside a fish suit.[7]

Mr. Temple was convinced that these hideous "abominations" were real. His reasoning for determining the reality of these creatures is based on what he understands of human nature. His reasoning was as follows:

"...the creatures credited with founding civilization in the Middle East were frankly described by the Babylonians who revered them and built huge statues of them as being *'repulsive abominations.'* If ever anything argued the authenticity of their account, it was this Babylonian tradition that the amphibians to whom they owed everything were disgusting, horrible, and loathsome to look upon. A more normal course for any invented tradition of the origins of civilization would have been to glorify the splendid gods or heroes who founded it. But instead we find specific descriptions of 'animals endowed with reason' who make their awed and thankful beneficiaries want to be sick with revulsion. And what is more, the tradition admits this freely!"

-Robert Temple
(The Sirius Mystery - 1976)

Confusion City

Edgar Cayce had implied that the hybrid creatures lacked intelligence. He had said that the Atlanteans who had migrated from Atlantis to Egypt before Atlantis sank had used them mostly as pets, or to do menial tasks. But was he again trying to hide something? Was Babylon, in fact, a civilization that was culturally founded by the "daughters of men"?

Besides what the Berossus fragment openly states about Oannes being a Musarus Annedotus, other clues that Babylon was, indeed, a civilization founded by the "daughters of men" can be found in the linguistic clues contained in the word "Babylon." By examining these linguistic clues, it becomes apparent that the word "Babylon" was not an arbitrary choice for the name of that ancient civilization.

Two versions of "The Musarus Oannes the Annedotus"

Unexplainably, there are two versions of Oannes. One is the fish suit type depiction (on the left). The other is a more traditional looking mermaid or merman look (on the right):upper torso is human looking, bottom half is a fishtail.

Robert Temple does not explain why there are two versions of Oannes. Our only guess is that here may be a rare instance where the depiction of a hybrid creature was, indeed, symbolic. The fish suit depiction seems much more dignified and majestic than the merman version. The drawings of Babylonian statues of Oannes were of the fish suit type version. Our guess is that the fish suit version was the symbolic version precisely because the merman version is more repulsive and the less dignified version. So that to a degree, Oannes was glorified in some of his depictions.

First linguistic clue: The root word in "Babylon" is "Babel." According to Robert Temple, to the ancient Jews, "Babel" meant "confusion." Even today, if one talks incoherently, she or he is said to "babble."

From Chapter 8, we know that "confusion" (as in "the lines of confusion") was one of the Anunnaki code words for the "daughters of men, "the hybrid creatures. In this case, understanding that the word "confusion" was a coded reference to the "daughters of men" is the key to unlocking several linguistic clues hidden in the word "Babylon," relative to the "daughters of men."

With that understanding, linguistically, we get that "Babel," or "confusion," is the root meaning of Babylon. Substituting this coded reference to the "daughters of men" for the root word "Babel," or "confusion," we now get that the "daughters of men" were the roots (or the root meaning) of Babylon.

Second linguistic clue: Zecharia Sitchin states that "Babylon" also means "gateway of the gods," and that the "gods" had a spaceport in Babylon. Implicit in the "gateway of the 'gods'" meaning is that the Anunnaki were letting us know that they had a presence in, and a knowledge of Babylon, and that they were keeping an eye on developments in Babylon.

Third linguistic clue: Another interesting observation on the word "Babylon," that I admit could be pure coincidence, is that the first part of the word "Babylon" is "baby." Suggesting, perhaps, yet another Anunnaki play on words, where some of the creatures of Babylon represented the baby or infantile forms of the human race--the pre-Adam forms.

Fourth linguistic clue: Once a-pun a time...I cannot say with certainty that this fourth linguistic clue was actually consciously intended by the Anunnaki either, but it is definitely a linguistic characteristic inherent in the word "Babylon." That is, the word "Babylon" is also a pun. With the "daughters of men" theme in mind, the word "Babylon" is a sharp witted pun poking a sardonic humor at the hybrid creatures and the humans who revered them. That pun is: "Babel on," as in, let the "confusion" continue.

Fifth linguistic clue: "Babylon" is a word with multiple meanings. The use of words with multiple meanings was a characteristic of the Anunnaki. It was practically their linguistic signature, their accent. That the word "Babylon" has multiple meanings and that these multiple meanings point to both the "daughters of men" and the extraterrestrials suggest that the Anunnaki may have actually named Babylon themselves, not the Amurru, and not Sargon I.

So, besides the Berossus fragment stating openly that Oannes was a Musarus Annedotus, the hard physical linguistic evidence that Babylon was, indeed, a civilization founded by the "daughters of men" appears to have been "hidden" in the very meanings of the word "Babylon" itself. A type of linguistic joke by the Anunnaki. A poetic, metaphorical message in a bottle that says in essence: *"This is Babylon. This is the city of the 'lines of confusion.' This is the culture that that race helped create and build. This is Confusion City, or the City of Confusion--Babylon."*

Universal Depictions

The problem of believing in the reality of the "daughters of men" (the pre-Adam humans) is understandable. Besides the eons of time that have pasted since these fantastic creatures actually walked the Earth, there have been no fossil remains found of them. Not a one, though Erich Von Daniken claims to have found several tombs of beings fifteen feet tall.

Though there is admittedly no fossil remains of these creatures, there is considerable graphic depictions of them on ancient walls, tomb paintings, sculptures, statues, and on pottery. These strange depictions can be found in most ancient cultures; in Sumer, Assyria, Babylon, ancient Egypt, ancient Rome, and ancient Greece, not to mention the strange depictions found in the Orient, and in India.

The Emperor's New Clothes

It seems to me that the ancient peoples of Sumer, Babylon, Assyria, Egypt, Rome and Greece were as proud of their civilizations as we are of ours. They did everything in their power, except leave us photographs, to try to show whoever came after what their civilizations were like. But we figure that they were too primitive to actually tell us the truth. We insist on putting our own interpretation on the artifacts and records they left us. We refuse to take the artifacts at face value.

Our refusal to accept the reality of the ancient depiction of these hybrid creatures is the "creation myth" syndrome all over again. It does not occur to us that the ancient depictions of these hybrid creatures were attempts at showing us exactly what the ancient peoples thought these creatures looked like. It does not occur to us that they were not being metaphorical. That they were not being symbolic. That they were not inventing mythologies. They were not trying to be enigmatic—depicting something that we could not understand. Just like the "creation myths," they were being as literal as they knew how to be.

But we have been conditioned, when looking at depictions of beings from antiquity, to believe that we do not see what we think we see. Or that what we see does not mean what we think it means. That only a trained and seasoned archaeologist or anthropologist can interpret what we think we are seeing.

When we see depictions of Seth, the dog-headed god of Egypt, we are led to believe that, well, that's not really what we are seeing. It doesn't really mean what it seems to mean--that the god Seth had the head of a dog. Or that Zu, in the ancient Sumerian texts, was actually a bird like creature, even though the ancient depictions of Zu show him as a one-eyed (Cyclops) bird-like creature. Or that the Sphinx, a frightening creature with the body of a lion, the wings of an eagle, and head of a man, a statue bigger than some apartment buildings, well, it doesn't really mean that there were creatures with the body of a lion, the wings of an eagle, and the face of a man. It doesn't mean that at all. It means...well that...they must have been into abstract art way back then, and well,...there was nothing better for those primitives to do with their time, there being no television, or any good movies to go see. No Disney World. So they made this really weird great big statue, that probably took them several hundred years just because...well, they had nothing better to do with their time. But you're not seeing what you think you're seeing.

In the well-researched book *Babylon* (1972), by the London writer James Wellard, we have a splendid example of this conditioning, as Mr. Wellard describes several elaborate, beautiful enameled wall ceramics or reliefs found on one of the walls of the Babylon excavation:

> "It is not surprising, then, that the enameled animals that adorn the Ishtar Gate and the Processional Way are really very beautiful and very pleasant to look upon. The yellow bulls on a blue background are splendid creatures, conceived in an entirely different style from the massive and forbidding winged bulls with human heads which guarded the royal palaces. One feels that they were meant to welcome and amuse the country pilgrims who came to Babylon for the festival of Marduk. Nor were the dragons, silver on blue, intended to frighten them for they are sprightly beasts, not dissimilar to a cheetah. In any case, this mythological beast whose ancestry must have gone back to prehistory before the giant lizards became extinct was the scared animal of Marduk..."[p.168]
>
> -James Wellard
> *(Babylon A History of the Greatest*
> *City of the Ancient World... - 1972)*

The assumption Mr. Wellard makes is traditional: that all the figures on this Babylonian wall are mythological. i.e., We are not seeing what we think we are seeing.[8]

Better Than a Photograph Or, How Big is the Sphinx?

Okay, they didn't have cameras way back then, but, then, again, they did know the nature of things that were perishable. Ironically, a photograph may not have survived 8,000 to 10,000 years (or more), even in the dry desert heat of the Nile. But a really, really big statue of one of the "daughters of men," that would be around for a long, long time.

Why would they leave us the Sphinx? If not ancient abstract art, what else could the Sphinx possibly represent? Try an unforgettable, impossible to explain in any other way--reality. Big as life. Bigger. A monument to the folly of humanity's infancy. A monument to a first cause, and a mysterious time never to be completely remembered, or completely forgotten.

Perhaps, they were trying to tell us that creatures like the Sphinx were real! And that they looked exactly like that gigantic statue they left us in Egypt!

We challenge any anthropologist or archaeologist to show us one passage out of the hundreds of thousands of ancient texts that have been translated that even hints that the ancient people thought these hybrid creatures were not real, that they were "mythological."

CHAPTER 10:
WHY THEY ARE HERE

"The Great Work is the transmutation of the gross forms of natural humanity into the perfected wise humanity."

-*Alchemy*

Short Term Objectives

When *UFOs* & *Extraterrestrials: Why They Are Here—The Darkest, Longest Kept Secret in Human History* was first published in 1996, we felt relatively certain we knew why the extraterrestrials were here. Based on a single cryptic paragraph found in *The Origin and Destiny of Man*, by Edgar Cayce, and the other evidence cited in this UFO study, it appeared they came to "rescue" the human life-essences trapped in the dream-body thought-form projections:

"Amilius, with the aid of spiritual-minded soul entities from other realms--'the sons of the Most High'-- intervened in this miss happened evolution which earth-man had created for himself."

-Edgar Cayce
(The Origin &Destiny of Man - 1972)

"Miss happened evolution that earthman had created for himself" was Cayce's phraseology for that early period when human life-essences projected their consciousness into three dimensional Earth reality in the dream- body thought-form projections—Lilith [the great owl], the Sphinx, the griffin, the mermaid, the unicorn, the satyr, the pegasus, the dragon, the serpent, etc.—and got trapped.[1] Once it was realized that Cayce was referring to the extraterrestrials (i.e., the "spiritual-minded soul entities from other realms"), it became fairly obvious why they became involved: To find a way to undo a dilemma of cosmic proportions. To get the entrapped human life-essences out of the congealed dream-bodies and back into the "homelands" of the higher vibrational realms, i.e., it was a "rescue mission."

Yet, that reason may be only the surface reason. It may not be the main reason, or the most important reason. There has apparently been a short-term objective of this extraterrestrial intervention that we had entirely overlooked in 1996.

To fully grasp this short-term objective, an analogy may help. Let's say, for example, you and someone you love dearly, perhaps, a spouse or your mate or one of your children, or a beloved parent or friend are hiking in the Rocky Mountains, in Colorado. The loved one slips and falls into a ravine, breaks a leg. Two hundred feet below, at the bottom of this ravine, you see that the loved one is alive, but in considerable pain. There is no easy way you can climb down and help them, and you don't have a rope. What do you do?

Or, a loved one is visiting a foreign country. Gets accused of being a drug dealer and ends up incarcerated in a jail in this foreign country. What do you do?

For one, you don't just forget about the loved one, or write them off. What you do, until you can actually get them out, is make them as comfortable as you can. In the case of the loved one trapped in the ravine, maybe you throw down your canteen and any can goods you have in your backpack. May be you throw down your knife or rifle, so that they can protect themselves. You may also throw down your flashlight, in case you don't make it back before dark. Then, after you've done all you can think to do to make things a little easier for your stricken loved one, you run for help.

In the case of the loved one wrongly incarcerated, maybe you make sure they have cigarettes or candy, fresh fruits and vegetables. You try to visit the jail frequently so the police and the guards know that someone crazy is concerned about this prisoner's welfare, who is your loved one. You get the best lawyer you can afford, and you and the lawyer(s) work towards the release of your beloved. Nothing else matters. You do everything in your power to make it as easy as you can for your incarcerated loved one.

These, metaphorically, have been the "short term" objectives of the extraterrestrials. These short term objectives have been so prevalent and omnipresent in humanity's evolution that it has been easy to overlook the love and the compassion these efforts represent, and just as easy to take these short term objectives for granted. But, they are not givens.

Just like the two hypothetical examples listed above, one of the subtle reasons they are here has been to improve the quality of human life, not in some hypothetical distant future, but at whatever point or level of human evolution they have observed us in, and in whatever ways they could think of. Make us a little more comfortable, while they try to figure out what exactly to do next, as they work toward our eventual release.

The creation of Adam represented a major effort in time, resources, and ingenuity and could realistically be seen as the initial attempt to improve the quality of human life, by changing the forms humans inhabited to one that could, at least, evolve intellectually and learn to appreciate art, beauty and culture. Relative to the quality of life, the Anunnaki made Adam as pragmatically and as beautifully as they could. They had actually believed that the four-armed, four-footed form would appeal to the new humans. They had wanted the race of Adam to like their new bodies and new faces, and to be happy in their new existence.

One of the findings that came out of Zecharia Sitchin's research in *The 12th Planet*, that quietly demonstrates this unspoken compassion the Anunnaki, at times, seem to have for humans was that despite the ancient texts saying that the "gods" called humans the "primitive worker," they did not think that the edible plants that existed on Earth, when the race of Adam were first created, would satisfactorily sustain humans. So, Enki, the God of Wrath and Wholesale Destruction, Butt-Kicker Extraordinaire, goes into his laboratory and genetically creates "apricots, cherries, onions, lentils, beans, cucumbers, cabbage, and lettuce. Milk was obtained from sheep, goats, and cows; from milk yogurt, butter, cream, and cheese. Breads, pastries, cakes, and biscuits were made from the grains."

Zecharia also claims that "there were technical manuals found on making beer from barley; wine was made from grapes and date palms." All of these healthy and good tasting fruits, vegetables, and recreational beverages were attempts by the "gods" to improve the quality of human life.

Teaching the ancient Sumerians how to perform cataract and brain surgery; teaching them the use of herbs and medicines to heal diseases; teaching them hygiene; how to build safer, stronger dwellings using bricks made with straw. These were all attempts to improve the quality of human existence.

That may also be why the "gods" taught Cro-Magnons rudimentary art and music. They were trying to cultivate a deeper appreciation of beauty and culture in primitive humans. *The appreciation of beauty, art and music are not essential to human survival, but they do greatly improve the "quality" of human life.* They refine it. They create joy, happiness, and contentment. An oil lamp to see by, a good meal, some music and some wine or beer, maybe a sing-a-long or two, that would have made life tolerable, 40,000 years ago, back in the French caves in Cro-Magnon, or 7,000 or 8,000 years ago, in some modest brick dwelling in Sumer.

The short-term goal has been to improve the quality of human life, a subtle yet necessary element of humanity's continued desire to live, perhaps, even more important in humanity's infancy than now.

Long Term Objectives

Logically, if such an alien "rescue mission" has actually existed, it would specifically address the causes of the "fall," or entrapment. Even though humans were no longer trapped in the dream-body thought-form projections,[2] they were still trapped in three-dimensional Earth reality, without an inkling of how to get out. The extraterrestrial's long-term objectives would logically focus on reversing the causes of entrapment.

These causes are not difficult to ascertain. The Cayce material actually names them:

The abuse of power: "As souls used and abused their privileges, the highest and the lowest applications of divine force were made."

A turning away from the Source: "The few who sought the way were given guidance, as it has always been given; the masses deliberately turned away, seeking fulfillment of their own desires. These became entrapped."

The desire for sexual intercourse with the animals: "They observed the sex life of the animals and wanted to experience it."

Loss of divine intelligence: An indirect result of entrapment may have been the loss of divine intelligence. The intelligence of the entrapped ones may have degenerated to that of the animals and creatures they had mimicked.

If such a rescue mission actually exist, these alleged causes of entrapment would be the logical areas of focus of their long-term objectives.

Is there any proof that steps have been taken by extraterrestrials that would have directly addressed the above listed causes of entrapment? We think so.

The Abuse of Power: How have the "gods" addressed the innate tendency of humans to abuse power? Instructing humans in the use of progressively more advanced and more complex technologies, tools, and sciences has served multiple purposes in the rescue mission's agenda, not the least of which has been giving humans varying degrees of power over which we must execute control.

Psychological distance from the animals: The ability to comprehend and use technologies quickly helped to distinguished humans from animals. Technology was a way to impress upon the human psyche that they were different and superior to the animals, whom they had, in the other incarnation, had sex and children with. *Technology, initially, made life easier and helped create a much-needed psychological distance from the animals and from the former incarnations as hybrid creatures.*

Though there have been accidental discoveries, the majority of the early technologies and inventions were introduced to humans by the "gods." The Sumerians openly admitted this.

Thinking capacity: Understanding technologies also helped to develop the intellect or thinking capacity. It was instrumental in understanding numbers, measurements, systems of mathematics and the ability to think in abstractions. The ability to think in abstractions is necessary to understand the concept of entrapment, freedom, morality, and create more advanced technologies. It would also strengthen the atrophied intellect of the new humans.

Leisure: Technologies created devices that saved labor. Labor saving devices and processes saved time and created leisure. Leisure was a necessary commodity if humans were to have time to create, to learn, as well as to contemplate abstract concepts like religion, morality, beauty, art, music, whatever. Leisure also enhances the quality of human life.

Control of power: With the evolution of the technologies of war, technology has served as training wheels for our ability to be in control of power and not always abuse it. For instance, the President of the United States of American could easily destroy the planet at any time by simply giving the order for nuclear destruction. Or those entrusted by our military and the militaries of other countries could also destroy the entire planet with the pushing of a few buttons. Yet, somehow, they do not do this.

Every one who owns a gun or a weapon is not a killer. Through technologies we are learning to have and, yet, to not abuse power.

The study of the nature of the universe: Technology leads to the study of science and the nature of the universe. In its own way, science is turning human consciousness towards contemplation of the Primal Source, i.e., toward contemplation of a Creator.

Scientists used to insist that there was no God, that the Big Bang and other scientific "realities" factored out the need for a God.

In the *Newsweek* feature article "Science Finds God," by Sharon Begley (July 20, 1998), Carl Sagan was quoted as saying, "there was nothing for a Creator to do," and every thinking person was therefore forced to admit "the absence of God."

Now some scientists are not so sure. They are finding riddles and paradoxes and insights that only make sense if there is a Supreme Intelligence--a Creator--a Cosmic Designer of the Cosmos.

For instance, scientists have discovered that if "the constants of nature--unchanging numbers like the strength of gravity, the charge of an electron and the mass of a proton--were the tiniest bit different, then atoms would not hold together, stars would not burn and life would never have made an appearance."[3]

This observation implies the question, Who fine tuned it? What force or intelligence established the constants?

Another scientific observation that has led scientists to seriously consider the reality of a Creator of the cosmos is that "humans invent abstract mathematics, basically making it up out of their imaginations, yet math magically turns out to describe the world...Greek mathematicians divided the circumference of a circle by its diameter, for example, and got the number pi,3.14159...Pi turns up in equations that describe sub-atomic particles, light and other quantities that have no observable connection to circles."[4]

From this mathematical axiom scientists concluded that "our minds, which invent mathematics, conform to the reality of the cosmos. We are somehow tuned in to its truths...this seems to be telling us that something about human consciousness is harmonious with the mind of God."[5]

The study of science and technologies has led some scientists to conclude that there may be a designer to the cosmos, after all.

By introducing technologies, something the "gods" have always been at home with, there has been great evolutionary progress in: 1) perceiving a difference and a superiority to animals; 2) problem solving and abstract thought; 3) understanding the nature of manifestations of energy and matter from a primal source; 4) training and practice at controlling power; and 5) leisure; time to create or think or simply enjoy life.

Technology has been a many faceted boon for humans, achieving both the long term objectives listed above, as well as the short term objective of greatly increasing the quality of human life. It is no wonder the extraterrestrials are so fond of it, and so fond of using it to help humans evolve.

Turning Away From the Source: All major religions seem to have been started directly by the "gods," or by their subordinates ("angels.")

In *Gods From Outer Space?*, Erich Von Daniken's research states that the *Kabalah* (perhaps the most famous mystical book of all time) was dictated by the "angels of God," (i.e., Anunnaki subordinates). In Zecharia Sitchin's translation of the ancient Sumerian texts *When Time Began*, he says:

"Indeed, *Kabalah* literally means 'that which was received.'" [p.19]

The Yoga handbook, the *Bhagavad-Gita*, was allegedly spoken to the warrior Arjuna, by his best friend--"God," in the form of Lord Krishna—one hour before the battle of Kuruksetra, where Arjuna was to fight his kinsmen to the death over an inheritance.

In the *Bhagavad-Gita As It Is*, by His Divine Grace A.C Bhaktivedanta Swami Prabnupada, we read:

"The Blessed Lord said: I instructed this imperishable science of yoga to the sun- god, Vivasvan, and Vivasvan instructed it to Manu." [p.xix]

What of the origins of Judaism and Christianity? In Zecharia Sitchin's book *Divine Encounters*, Mr. Sitchin asks the question:

"So, who was Yahweh? Was He one of *them?* Was He an extraterrestrial?

"...The question and its implied answer, indeed, arise inevitably. That the biblical creation narrative with which the Book of Genesis begins draws upon the Mesopotamian *Enuma elish* is beyond dispute. That the biblical *Eden* is a rendering of the Sumerian E.DIN is almost self- evident. That the tale of the Deluge and Noah and the ark is based on the Akkadian *Atra-Hasis* texts and the earlier Sumerian Deluge tale in the *Epic of Gilgamesh*, is certain. That the plural 'us' in the creation of *The Adam* segments reflects the Sumerian and Akkadian record of the discussions by the leaders of the Anunnaki that led to the genetic engineering that brought *Homo sapiens* about, should be obvious."[p.347]

-Zecharia Sitchin *(Divine Encounters)*

Mr. Sitchin was convinced that Yahweh was, in fact, Enki, the Anunnaki commander, engineer, and genetic scientist. Among his other evidence he sites that one of Enki's many titles was "NU.DIM.MUD," "He who fashions things," and that the biblical prophets often referred to Yahweh [Enki] as "The Fashioner of Adam (not 'creator')".

If this is true, these beings also gave the world Judaism and Christianity, as well as the *Kabalah* and yoga (The *Bhagavad-Gita*).

I do not know Islam well enough to know its source. My understanding is that the prophet Mohammed received the Koran from either God or angels.

Were all of the world's major religious doctrines and philosophies started by or given to humans by the extraterrestrials? If so, that would fit part of the rescue plan's mission-- attempting to turn the "fallen angels" consciousness back to the contemplation of the Creator/Creatress, and contemplation of the moral consequences of action and thought: abstract concepts that would be necessary to evolve, and return to the consciousness of the pre-hybrid state of existence.

Desire for sexual intercourse: The human desire for sexual intercourse has been a major thorn in the side of the "gods" since they initially began the rescue mission millenniums ago.

There can be little doubt that our sexual morality came from the extraterrestrials. Our evidence of this is that the source of our present day sexual morality can be traced to the books of Leviticus. In Leviticus, we have the laws the "Lord" gave Moses and the Levite priests to give to the Hebrew people. The laws covered many topics, some concerning physical hygiene, some concerning payments of debts, some concerned social issues, and some concerned sexual attitudes, i.e., sexual morality. For example:

"And he shall take a wife in her virginity."
(Leviticus 21:13)

"They shall not take a wife that is a whore, or profane; neither shall they take a woman put away from her husband: for he is holy unto his God." (Leviticus 21:7)

The extraterrestrials were actually the first Puritans, or the inspiration for the Puritans. It was the extraterrestrials that institutionalized marriage, who introduced the concept of virginity and placed a great value on it. They were seeking psychological ways to curtail sexual activity among humans.

Remember, they had initially sought to do away with the need for sexual intercourse with another being altogether by creating the race of Adam as androgynous creatures. That plan, however, was one of their first major failures. They had to allow some form of sexual intercourse. There was simply no way around it, so they tried to narrow acceptable sexual behavior down to only having sex with your wives once you were married. The idea was to make sexual intercourse next to impossible to obtain outside of wedlock.

Initially, they tried polygamy, delighted that they could keep the sexual activity mostly inner species. If you doubt that forcing humans to have sex with only other humans and not with animals 3,000 or 4,000 years ago, was not a serious problem, Erich Von Daniken points out in *Gods From Outer Space?* that Moses repeatedly warned the Jews to not have sexual intercourse with animals. Von Daniken sites Leviticus 18:23 as the proof of this:

> "Neither shalt thou lie with any beast to defile thyself therewith: neither shall any woman stand before a beast to lie down thereto: it is confusion.
> Defile ye not yourselves in any of these things; for in all these the nations are defiled which I cast out before you:"

Because this was such a serious problem with all nations, not just the Jews, fornicating with animals was considered a capital offense. Von Daniken sites Leviticus 20:15-16 as evidence of this:

"And if a man lie with a beast, he shall surely be put to death; and ye shall slay the beast.

And If a woman shall approach unto any beast, and lie down thereto, thou shalt surely kill the woman, and the beast: they shall surely be put to death."

How serious was this problem? How much a part of the human sexual psyche was bestiality? If you think this was only a problem of the "ancient" peoples living in antiquity, that simply is not the case. When I was in my teens, not that many years ago, the original name for pornographic movies was "stag films." I'm not completely sure why there were called stag films. It might have been because some of these 8mm movies would show people having sexual intercourse with animals. There may have been different types of animals involved, but the only one I actually saw, during my self education on sex, was a woman having intercourse with a pony and some cartoons of men having sex with pigs, cows, or sheep. This is not a criticism. We are only pointing out that as recently as 30 or 40 years ago, humans were still fornicating with animals, and capturing it on film or in photographs.

The Anunnaki next introduced monogamy, in an effort to gradually wean humans from their sexual addiction. All the sexual laws found in Leviticus shifted, but remained primarily the main stay of our sexual morality.

Monogamy has only been marginally successful in controlling or limiting sexual activity among humans. The extraterrestrials are still searching for answers on how to break human sexual addiction, however. The present system is not working as they intended. It is, in fact, warping and creating more sex offenders, sexual perverts, and sexual murderers than it is creating sexually adjusted humans.

In truth, the extraterrestrials do not fully understand human sexuality. They never did.

Summary

The proof of the reality of UFOs and extraterrestrials can be found in anthropology, archaeology, in the *Enuma elish* (the ancient Sumerian "creation myth"), the codes found in Genesis, and the manner in which Genesis has been edited. (See Part II. The Genesis Conspiracy)

For proof of the reality of UFOs and extraterrestrials, remember the evolutionary timeline. Remember the "missing links," and the mysterious gaps in the understanding of human evolution that our best scientific minds can only guess at. Remember Lilith, the "Great Owl," the forerunner of Eve, and the "hairy ones" (the "demons"). Remember Sumer and the amazing technological advancements of a people who lived 5,000 to 8,000 years ago. Remember the Genesis codes ("daughters of men," "sons of God," and the "creeping thing"). Remember Moses warning the Jews that the penalty for fornicating with animals was death. Remember the mistakes! Remember the failures—that Adam wasn't supposed to want to have sex with any other creature, but that he did; that *The First Book of Enoch* never made it into the Bible because it contradicted the official cover-story the "gods" wanted to promote; that Adam was a hermaphrodite, with alluring feminine features; that Adam's sexual intercourse with the "daughters of men" (the hybrid creatures) resulted in the birth of genetic mutations—a race of giants—some of whom were worshipped as Greek and Roman "gods"; Apollo, Athena, Poseidon, Zeus, etc; and above all remember that the extraterrestrials, the Anunnaki, were not "gods," and that their very fallibility is the ultimate proof of their mortality and actual flesh and blood existence. And that we are here is also proof that they are here.

The mistakes and failures they made, and their simultaneous attempts to conceal yet preserve clues to these mistakes and failures is itself a curious pattern—a signature of sort--that betrays their existence.

A Mystery

And finally, there is a mystery here, a deep mystery. The aliens don't seem to want us to know these origins. The question is why? Were they initially afraid if we knew, we would be overcome with grief at what we had done, and the hundreds, perhaps thousands of lifetimes of trial and error it would take to undo? Did they fear that we would harbor a grudge at how they frequently destroyed those of us they thought were "unclean?" Were they afraid that we would revert back to our former sexual perversions if we knew? Or did the knowledge of who and what we once were simply fade into the realm of myth and discover and have tried to present here, they have been terribly wrong on more than one occasion about how we would respond. We think they were wrong on this one as well. And yet, how could they have told us? Who would have believed them?

How can you hit an evolutionary target that you don't even know exist?

We welcome your input on this topic. Please send insights and thoughts to:

elliotthughes777@gmail.com

THE GENESIS CONSPIRACY

You are the devil's gateway...You are she who persuaded him whom the devil did not dare attack...Do you not know that you are each an Eve? The sentence of God lives on in this age; the guilt, necessarily, lives on too."

-Tertullian

Early Christian minister writing about 180 A.D.

Why was Genesis edited? How were the meanings and interpretations changed? And to what end?

The answer to these questions prove the flesh and blood reality of extraterrestrials, and that extraterrestrials have been an omnipresent influence in the creation and evolution of the human species since its beginnings.

How Were The Meanings Changed?

We can obtain our first clues by simply comparing the texts of the original Sumerian version of the creation of Adam (called the *Enuma elish*) with a more recent King James version of the Bible. Then, simply noting the differences that we detect. Let's summarize the original Sumerian version first:

Synopsis of the *Enuma elish*
(The Original Version of Genesis)

1. A group of 600Anunnaki land in the waters of the Persian Gulf. There are male and female officers and flight crew members.

2. They began mining gold in the waters of the Persian Gulf.

3. The gold mining process is deemed too slow. There is a change in command. It is decided that mining gold in south African mines will be more productive.

4. The flight crew is chosen to be the miners. After 144,000 earth years of being miners, the flight crew mutiny.

5. After a conference, the Anunnaki command decide to make a *lulu--a* "primitive worker" (Man)-- to replace the striking flight crew members. This discussion was fragmented and placed in Genesis in the passage: *"Let us make man in our own image, etc."* (Gen.1:26)

6. An alien female scientist named Ninhursag begins the initial groundbreaking genetic experiments that will produce the "primitive worker."

7. Later, Ninhursag is joined by her husband, Enki, who is also a genetic scientist, as well as an engineer and a commanding officer. Together they "fashion" "The Adam," or "Model Man."

8. About a dozen or so Anunnaki women are artificially inseminated with the zygotes of the new race of Adam. They carry the embryos 10 months to term in their own wombs then give birth to the new race of Adam.

"The primitive worker," Adam, is put to work in the mines and in the Garden of Eden.

That's a summation of the *Enuma elish*—the original, ancient Sumerian version of how and why Adam was created.

Let's now look at a summary of Genesis and see if we can spot the changes.

Synopsis of the Genesis Version of the Creation of Adam

1. A single God creates the cosmos. (Gen.1:1)
2. This singular God decides to make Man as a sort of crowning touch to the other creations.
3. After briefly discussing the issue with Himself (or with angels), this singular God creates Adam from the clay or mud of the earth, breathes the breath of life into Adam, and Adam is now a living being. (Gen.1:26)
4. After an undetermined time, God decides that Adam needs a "helpmate." Puts Adam to sleep, and creates Eve from one of Adam's ribs. (Gen.2:22)
5. Shortly after Eve is created, she allows herself to be misled by a serpent. She disobeys God by eating the apple, and offers the apple to Adam. (Gen. 3:1 -6)
6. When God returns and ask Adam and Eve how they knew that they were naked, Adam claims that he is blameless and spinelessly says it is all Eve's fault. (Gen. 3:11-12)
7. They are both expelled from the Garden of Eden, and because of Eve's folly, all humans must now be born in what is called "original sin." (Gen. 3:23 -24)
8. The rest is history as we know it.

Spin

What were the changes, and how do they change the meaning of the story?

Change #1. From pantheon to a singular deity: In the *Enuma elish* (the original texts), there was an official "family" of the "gods" -the husbands, wives, the children and grandchildren of the commanding officers. We may think of the commanding officers and their families as royalty, the Anunnaki flight crew members were considered "angels" of the "gods," which originally meant "emissaries" of "god."

In antiquity, any of the commanding (ruling) family members would have been considered legitimate "gods." This would have obviously included the Anunnaki women, who would have been worshipped, legitimately as "goddesses." Ishtar/ Inanna and Isis, just to name a couple, were, indeed, Anunnaki women of the commanding officers' families (the royal family) who were worshipped as "goddesses."

In Genesis, we have gone from a pantheon of many legitimate "gods" and "goddesses" to one "god." Why? What does this change do to how the story is interpreted? *By editing out the pantheon, God is now perceived as only masculine.* This indirectly elevates the status of all males, since God is now only of their sex. Eliminating the pantheon eliminates *all* female "goddesses" in a single stoke of the pen.

Change #2. The reason man is created is elevated: In Genesis, the reason for Man's creation has been elevated in importance and· status. In the *Enuma elish*, Man is created as a "primitive worker," a mere lackey to the "gods." In Genesis, however, Man is created as the crowning touch, the coupe de gras of God's created universe. Man is given "dominion" over all things. *In Genesis, Man has gone from a mere lackey/miner to the "gods," to a prince of God.*

Change #3. No specific mention of the creation of women: In the *Enuma elish*, there is no specific mention of the creation of women. In itself, this is quite interesting, for either women were created at the same time, or, as fuels our earlier hypothesis the first genetically engineered humans were hermaphrodites--male *and* female. That would explain why the original texts makes no specific mention of the creation of women— there were as yet neither separate women nor separate men, only the dual-sexed hermaphrodites.

In Genesis, Eve (womankind) is created to be Adam's "helpmate." Her punishment for listening to the serpent is (among other things) that*...thy husband shall RULE over thee"*:

> *"Unto the woman he said, I will greatly multiply thy sorrow and thy conception; in sorrow thou shalt bring forth children; and thy desire shall be to thy husband, and he shall rule over thee."*(Gen. 3:16)

Woman is created second, after males, as a sort of afterthought, and she is only created to help Adam. That is her only stated purpose. In Genesis, womankind has taken Man's place as "primitive worker" or lackey, but not to the "gods," but to Adam (mankind).

Change #4. Women no longer had a hand in creating Adam: In the *Enuma elish*, an alien female scientist named Ninhursag begins the initial groundbreaking genetic experiments that lead to the "fashioning" of the "primitive worker." Enki joins her efforts later, and together they "fashion" Adam.

In the original version, Anunnaki women carried the first experimental humans 10 months to term, in their own wombs, to incubate the experimental human embryos. There was great joy and excitement when the first of the race of Adam were born to the Anunnaki surrogate mothers.

In Genesis, the Anunnaki women ("goddesses") birthing the first humans is edited out of the texts entirely. Again, "God" is singular, masculine, and He creates Adam without the least bit of help from anyone or anything.

The Power of Myth

What are the overall effects of this edited Genesis version? The society we have before us, where men rule and women (females) are accountable to their fathers, husbands, brothers, or lovers, and are considered all but the "property" of males is the result.

The Bible now becomes justification for this sexual, social structure because biblically, God is now strictly masculine. Eve's folly is now the reason we all suffer and are born in "original sin." There are no longer "goddesses" for females to turn to for justice or retribution, if they feel mistreated or powerless. They must pray to a male deity, one of the enemy, one of those who oppresses them.

On the other hand, biblically, man's status has been elevated from that of "primitive worker" or "lackey to the gods," to prince and darling of God, until Eve causes the expulsion. "Darn Eve" (we are encouraged to think). Because women were now created second, after Adam (God's obvious first choice in what sex should rule), and because women (Eve) were the first to disobey God and ruin it for the rest of us, we must conclude from the Genesis version of creation that it is only just and right that women have such an unjust and hard lot. We conclude from this Genesis version that it is their own fault, and besides, who are we males to argue the judgment of God?

That is the social-psychological effect of the Genesis edited version of creation on the social status and position of women and men in our society. In light of this Genesis re- interpretation, it is no wonder Jewish men give a daily thank you prayer to God that they were not born female.

Now that we see the summaries side by side, with out much effort it is easy to see that the edited version of Genesis dramatically reduces the status of women, removes the support of the "goddesses" they once prayed to for help and blames women for the suffering of the entire species of humans. It is not difficult to deduce that Genesis is a subtle and cunning form of punishment against all females. Which brings us to the most obvious of questions, why? Who would have the wisdom, power and authority to so effect women's social status, and why? To what end?

If the primary sources of Genesis were not believed to be the "word of God," it would be very easy to believe that whoever edited Genesis had a deep and all pervasive hatred for all females; a hatred so immense that it would make the misogamy of a Jack the Ripper, or a Boston Strangler pale by comparison of its depth of passion. Since we do not attribute such a strong, passionate hatred as being part of the psychological make up of God, we are baffled as to what mean-spirited individual would edit a religious document with such blatant and cunning hatred for one half of the human species. Instead of clarity, this revelation only deepens the mystery.

And how does the edited version of the creation of Adam in Genesis prove the reality of extraterrestrials? It is proof in that it bares their signature. The very motivation and cunning for this apparently mean-spirited act implicates them.

Whodunit?

By this we mean that we are left with only two possible choices in regard to who edited Genesis to be a subtle attack on all females: Either these changes in Genesis were the direct wishes of "God," or the Levite priests (who compiled the books of the Bible at around 1000 BC) took it upon themselves to change the texts and the meaning of the story of creation of Adam, to diminish women's social status.

The problem with that line of reasoning is that, according to Zecharia Sitchin's analysis of both the ancient Sumerian texts and the Bible, the Levite priests were exceptionally loyal to the wishes and directions of Yahweh (Enki). The Levite priests were given the laws by God, and they passed these laws onto the Jewish people. They appeared to attempt to do the Lord's will in all things, both important and mundane.

So if the Levite priests compiled the books of the Bible, we can be fairly certain that they did it precisely as Yahweh instructed.

If the Levite priests didn't take it upon themselves to edit Genesis with this anti-feminine slant, then, we are left with the conclusion that it was Yahweh (Enki) himself, and perhaps, the other ruling members of the Anunnaki high command that made the decision to edit Genesis with the anti-female slant.

When we realize that it was "The Lord"--God--who stacked the deck against women, we are baffled and confused. Does not "The Lord" love all of his creatures, males and females? Why the overt favoritism? Why would "God" have such a passionate hatred of women?

The Tip of the Iceberg

Yet, there is much more. Sick and numb with disbelief, we discover that the edited version of Genesis is but the tip of a horrific iceberg.

While studying the early religions of the first humans, it becomes clear that, originally, both "goddesses" and "gods" were worshipped with equal respect. Both "goddess" and "god" worshipping religions had both male and female followers. Goddess worshipping religions, or evidence of them goes back 9,000 to 10,000 years.

In *When God Was A Woman* (1976), Merlin Stone cites several factors that support her contention that people in antiquity practiced goddess worship, not as a cult, but as a major religion. Quoting Margaret Mead, Leonard Cottrai and other anthropologists, Merlin points out that before primitive humans had made the connection between coitus and having children, women were believed to "miraculously" bring forth life. This anthropological observation coupled with the predominant appearance of little "Venus" statuettes (small stone and bone carvings of a pregnant woman, with no face) indicate that "goddess" worship was wide spread in ancient times.

However, there are strong indications that "goddess" worshippers may have participated in ritualistic sexual intercourse. It is not clear whether these ritualistic sexual practices involved animals, but if the golden calf created by the Jews during their exodus from Egypt is a clue, they may very well have sanctified sexual intercourse with animals. If that was indeed the case, it would help to explain the wrath of Yahweh (Enki), and the ruthless, merciless campaign that was launched about 7,000 BC that eventually destroyed all traces of Goddess worship.

It is difficult to reconcile that the same beings that compassionately genetically engineered and birthed humans, also ordered the wholesale slaughter and destruction of women, children and old people. But this solution, in itself, may suggests a desperation on the part of the "gods" that we may never fully comprehend. It is horrible to contemplate, and yet these "God" ordained killings happened.

In *When God Was A Woman*, we read:

"The words and threats of Ezekiel, as well as the other prophets, were translated into murder and destruction, explained as having been commanded by Yahweh (Enki). They are recorded in this way in the pages of the Old Testament:

> "And the Lord said unto him, 'Go through the midst of Jerusalem and set a mark upon the foreheads of the men that sigh and that cry for all the abominations that are done in the midst thereof." And to the others he said in mine hearing, "go ye after him through the city and smite. Slay utterly, both old and young, both maids and little children and women, but come not near any man upon whom is the mark; and begin at my sanctuary." Then they began at the ancient men who were before the house. And he said unto them, "defile the house and fill the courts with the slain; go ye forth." And they went forth and they slew in the city." [Ezek. 9:4 - 7].

Merlin Stone gives many more examples of the cold blooded killings and massacres committed in the name of Yahweh, to suppress goddess worship. There's no reason to include more examples, we get the idea.

Our only clue as to why "The Lord" so willingly ordered these cold blooded murders is the use of the word "abominations." The "abomination" that has consistently ticked off the Anunnaki was humans fornicating with animals.

Apparently, the prophets could not convince the worshippers of the goddess religions to give up the practice of ritualistic sexual intercourse with animals. Threats and warnings had not worked. So, Yahweh (Enki) had them all massacred. Then, logically, began re-thinking how to keep humans from fornicating with animals, and how to break their sexual addiction.

Not "Gods"

The other key piece of evidence that ties this all together is that, as we have stated repeatedly, the Anunnaki were not "gods." By this we mean all we need do to know what they were really like is to look at ourselves. We are, after all, literally, their genetic offspring. We are the daughters and sons of the "gods. "We are like them--warlike, loving technology, quick to fight, converting power, loving the arts and music, passionate and sensuous. Loving our children and families and friends. Hating our enemies. Their degree of emotional control may have been only slightly higher than ours.

What we are postulating is the only remaining puzzle piece that makes sense. Namely, that Enki (Yahweh), the being primitive humans believed to be "God," harbored a grudge! "Vengeance is mine," Not being a "god," he was furious over his failures. Livid.

The first major failure was the race of Adam. Anunnaki women he knew intimately had birthed these first humans. Not only did they not like their four armed, four footed bodies, but they defied Enki ("God") and had sex with the animals and the mixtures. True, Enki and Ninhursag were the scientists that genetically engineered the hermaphrodites. Enki, of all people, knew that the race of Adam were NOT women, per se. Yet, they LOOKED like women. That's what stuck in his mind. His neuro-associations must have been that, yes, consciously, he knows the race of Adam were males and females--but the beauty of the creatures and that they defied him is what stayed in his mind.

The second failure was that his flight crew then mutinied--left him for the very creatures that he and his wife had genetically engineered. Again, feminine beauty is the neuro-association, they were still hermaphrodites at this point—but their beauty is why his men deserted him. The very beauty of the creatures he had created cost him the lives of 200 of his crew men. We can be relatively certain that the flood didn't claim the crew men who mutinied.

Failure number 3: Adam was split into male and female beings, and the "goddess" religions (mostly female priestesses and female followers) again defied his commands by having ritualistic sexual intercourse with animals. That was it. Gloves off. No holds barred. The game goes to level three.

Now, in all fairness, I do not understand why the Anunnaki did not simply quit. This would have been a pretty good place to simply throw in the old towel. Destroy us all, and be done with it. Then plot a course back to the home planet. But they've never quit on us. This is something that I truly do not understand. All we've ever been to them is trouble, and yet, they've never quit on us. They continue to try to evolve us. Help us. Why is not completely clear.

Level Three

At this point in the evolution of the human species, the Anunnaki are at wits end. Everything they have tried so far has blown up in their face, and they must feel that they are running out of options. How to keep humans from fornicating with animals, and how to limit their sexual activity all together are still their number one concerns.

What they ended up with was a solution that would both give Enki (and the Anunnaki command) a much needed, satisfying measure of revenge, and a psychological means to finally be able to control human sexual behavior to a much, much greater degree.

This is how the psychological reasoning went: The Anunnaki postulated that as long as men and women were both perceived as equals, there was no sexual accountability. No sexual guilt. Therefore, to control sexual behavior, women were cast in an inferior and subservient light in Genesis. Not that women were in any way inferior, but this slant best served the purpose of the plan. Because they were cast in this inferior and subservient light to males, they became, in essence, the "property" of their fathers, husbands, or brothers who would "protect" their virginity with their lives.

The beauty of this solution was that it also gave the Anunnaki a measure of revenge over human females (or the feminine aspect of the hermaphrodites), who had defied them in the past. Like many things the Anunnaki wrote or did, this solution was multi-dimensional.

Now, all the changes in Genesis begin to make sense. It wasn't just about revenge, though that was, indeed, part of it. The editing of Genesis, with the anti-feminine slant was a master psychological plan to further limit sexual intercourse among all humans, women and men. By making men "responsible" for "their" women, and making women subservient to men, the Anunnaki have established the most successful psychological control mechanism of human sexuality to date.[2]

The psycho-sociological pressure of Genesis is that, if you're a male, you don't let just anyone sleep with your mother, sister, your wife, or your daughter, if you can help it. You don't want them calling them a whore or a slut. If you're female, it's hard not to feel intimidated, or not to feel the unspoken pressure of having your friends or co-workers or classmates think you're a slut, or a whore. And because fewer females are willing to be labeled slut or whore, fewer males will have opportunity to have sexual intercourse with them. See how effective Genesis has been? Because most women do not want to be perceived as sluts or whores, there are fewer women to have sex with. Or, at least, there will be fewer sex partners. It's not perfect, and, as mentioned earlier, this puritanical sexual morality is creating more sexual perverts, more pedophiles, more sexual rape, insanity and murder than any sexual paradigms that have gone before it, but it has still been the most effective ploy they've tried so far.

We submit that the editing of Genesis with the intent of making women subservient to men, in order to control or psychologically limit the sexual behaviors of humans, and to exact a degree of revenge on females, is empirical evidence of the reality of extraterrestrials and of extraterrestrial intervention in the creation and evolution of the human species. It is the only answer that completely addresses the manner in which Genesis was edited--re-written.

Not Those Guys From E.DIN

"Now: In the beginning, there was not God the Father, Allah, Zoroaster, Zeus, or Buddha.

In the beginning there was instead, once more, a divine psychological gestalt—and by that I mean a being whose reality escapes the definition of the word 'being,' since it is the source from which all being emerges...

"Nor was the universe created for one species alone, by a God who is simply a super vision of the same species—as willful and destructive as man at his worst.

Instead, you have an inner dimension of activity, a vast field of multidimensional creativity, a Creator that becomes a portion of each of its creations, and yet a Creator that is greater than the sum of its parts: a Creator that can know itself as a mouse in a field, or as the field, or as the continent upon which the field rests, or as the planet that holds the continent, or as the universe that holds the world—a force that is whole yet divisible, that is one and the inconceivably many, a force that is eternal and mortal at once, a force that plunges headlong into its own creativity, forming the seasons and experiencing them as well, glorifying in individuation, and yet always aware of the great unity that is within and behind and through all experiences of individuality: a force from [which] each moment pasts and futures flow out in every conceivable direction."

-Jane (Seth) Roberts
(Dreams, "Evolution," and Value Fulfillment - 1986)

SOURCES

Cayce, Edgar. 1976. *The Origin and Destiny of Man*. Avon Books.

Corso, Philip J. Col. [Ret.] 1996. *The Day After Roswell*. Pocket Books.

Diamond, Jared. 1992. *The Third Chimpanzee*. HarperPerennial.

Hamblin, Dora Jane. 1973. *The First Cities*. Time-Life Books.

Hamilton, Edith. 1940. *Mythology Timeless Tales of Gods and Heroes*. A Mentor Book.

Montgomery, Ruth. 1976. *The World Before*. Ballantine Books.

Montgomery, Ruth. 1985. *Aliens Among Us*. Ballantine Books.

Oates, Joan. 1996. *Babylon Revised Edition*. Thames and Hudson.

Pagels, Elaine. 1995. *The Origin of Satan*. Random House.

Prabhupada, A.C. Bhaktivedanta, Swami. 1968. *Bhagavad-Gita As It Is*. International Society for Krishna Consciousness.

Roberts, Jane. 1986. *Dreams, Evolution, and Value Fulfillment*. Prentis Hall Press.

Ryan, Donald P. 1999. *The Complete Idiot's Guide to Lost Civilizations*. Alpha Books.

Sitchin, Zecharia. 1976. *The 12th Planet*. Avon Books.

Sitchin, Zecharia. 1985. *The Wars of Gods and Men*. Avon Books.

Sitchin, Zecharia. 1996. *Divine Encounters*. Avon Books.

Stone, Merlin. 1976. *When God Was a Woman*. A Harvest/HBJ Book.

Streiber, Whitley. 1987. *Communion*. Wilson and Neff, Inc.

Streiber, Whitley. 1990. *Majestic*. Penguin Putman.

Swartz, Howard. 1988. *Lilith's Cave*. Oxford University Press.

Temple, Robert K.G. 1976. *The Sirius Mystery*. Destiny Books.

Von Daniken, Erich. 1968. *Gods From Outer Space*. A Bantam Book.

Wellard, James. 1972. *Babylon A History of the Greatest City of the Ancient World and Its Rediscovery by Modern Archaeologists*.

PARTING THOUGHT

I n Samuel Kramer's book *From the Tablets of Sumer* (1956), Kramer mentions how the biblical story of *Job* was originally a Sumerian tale. According to Kramer, the storylines (the morals) have identical meanings. That moral is: *"in the case of* [human] *suffering and adversity, no matter how seemingly unjustified, the victim has but one valid and effective recourse, and that is to glorify his god continually, and keep wailing and lamenting before him until he turns a favorable ear to his prayer."*

The thing that has always bothered me about the biblical story of Job is that the name looks phonetically like the word "job," as in "get a job," or, "I have a job." The biblical name "Job," in order to be pronounced "Jobe," should have an "e" on the end of it, but it doesn't. And I'd be willing to bet that the first time anyone sees the biblical spelling of "Job" the natural inclination is to think it's pronounced "job." There is a brief moment of mental resistance as we adjust and think, "Okay, the correct pronunciation of this word is "Jobe." But there persist a subliminal, fundamental wrongness with pronouncing J-O-B "Jobe." I mean, come on, it's not like trying to pronounce the name "Nebuchadnezzar." [Neb-bah-ka-nezzer]. It's a three letter word, for Pete's sake.

So what? What's the big deal?

Well, maybe they're playing another mind-game with us--as in "*Lulus*, you primitive workers, this is your Jobe [i.e. job]. Or, "the story of Job is your job?" Or, "to be like Job is the job of the primitive worker?"

Are they making fun of us, or is sardonic humor just their compulsive way to communicate with humans? Of course, another possibility is that they communicated with humans with metaphor, puns, and words and phrases with multiple meanings so that certain meanings or messages couldn't be edited out of tales because the hidden meaning escapes the editors?

ENDNOTES

Chapter 1. End Notes:

1. Jared Diamond, *The Third Chimpanzee*, 1992.
2. *Ibid.*
3. *Ibid.*
4. *Ibid*
5. *Ibid.*
6. Quite interestingly, this exact pattern happens again in regard to the Norsemen—the Vikings. They seemed to have come out of nowhere. See *When God Was a Woman* (1976), by Merlin Stone.

Chapter 2. End Notes:

1. *The 12ᵗʰ Planet*, by Zecharia Sitchin, (1976)
2. *Ibid*
3. **Bitumen:** a black sticky substance obtained from petroleum, used for covering roads, etc.: bitumen coal; coal that burns with a smokey flame.
4. *The 12ᵗʰ Planet*, by Zecharia Sitchin, (1976)
5. *Ibid*

Chapter 3. End Notes:

1. ***Shars:*** That there was a formal designation for this

3,600 year cycle is a type of empirical evidence of the reality of this species of extraterrestrial life forms, in that 8,000 years ago, in a civilization that had not yet learned to count to 10, who would bother converting Earth time into derivatives of 3,600 year cycles, and to what end? It only made sense if the beings stationed on Earth wanted to know what time (or year) it was and back on their home planet. Just as one of us traveling to another country would simultaneously keep that country's time, and know approximately what time it was back in the states.

2. **Divine Dreams:** Metaphysical lore holds that the power of the Creator/Creatress' mind is so vast that Her/His thoughts thought thoughts , and those thoughts thought thoughts, and those thoughts thought thoughts. These "generations" of thoughts were called "Logos.".

Chapter 4. End Notes:

1. I was discussing this idea with a friend, who is a nurse, and she matter of fact said that "even in these modern times, there are perhaps 1 out of 1000 babies born that are true hermaphrodites (infants born with both a penis and a vagina)." The nurse said the normal procedure was to amputate the penis and make them girls. It was easier and the children were never told.

2. **Lilith:** The Jewish explanation of this seemingly androgynous origin of Adam holds that Gen. 1:27 is a reference to the creation of "Lilith." This interpretation , however, may have served a duel purpose. It may have

been an attempt to make those biblical passages more understandable. It may also have serviced as a psychological device to keep Jewish women their place, since "Lilith," according to this interpretation leaves Adam because she did not want to be on the "bottom," a submission position during sexual intercourse.

3. The following quote was discovered after this revised edition was already typeset: "*Male and female created he them ; and blessed them , and called **their** name Adam, in the day they were created.*" (Gen. 5:2) And called their name Adam!

"*And Adam lived an hundred and thirty years, and begat a son in his own likeness, after his image; and called his name Seth.*" (Gen. 5:3)

Chapter 5. End Notes:

1. *The 12ᵗʰ Planet*, by Zecharia Sitchin, (1976)
2. *Ibid.*
3. *Ibid.*
4. You just about need a bag of popcorn and a scorecard to keep up with the various sources and types of creatures and monstrosities roaming Earth during this period. By our count you had:
   a) The pure entrapped creatures in the thought-form projected dream bodies—Lilith and the gang.
   b) The offspring of the entrapped creatures with animals.
   c) The offspring of the entrapped creatures with each other.

d) The offspring of the Anunnaki flight crew members, who mutinied, with the race of Adam.

e) The offspring of the Anunnaki who mated with hybrid creatures.

5. *The Secret Doctrine*, by H.P. Blavatsky, (1880)

6. *The Third Chimpanzee*, by Jared Diamond.

DNA backdating placing Adam at 288,000 years ago and Eve at 255,000 to 275,000 years ago also lends credence to the theory that Adam was an androgynous. For either the race of Adam were androgynous or Adam went mateless for from 13,000 to 33,000 years (not including sex with the mixtures, sex with the muting members of the Anunnaki, and sex with animals.)

Chapter 6. End Notes:

1. *The 12ᵗʰ Planet*, by Zecharia Sitchin.

2. According to Ruth Montgomery's Guides, the mixtures were also called "things."—*The World Before.*

3. *The 12ᵗʰ Planet*, by Zecharia Sitchin.

4. "It is also worth mentioning the statement *in the* Cabala that originally human beings did not look each other in the face during the sex act and that **the union of the seed took place in a single being.** Modern Cabalists claim that, before Adam, God created another being who was man only, a characteristic that did not prevent this being from producing children, who later mated with the snake." [p. 135-136] *Gods From Outer Space.* 1970. By Erich Von Daniken.

The "being before God created Adam" was Adam before Adam was genetically split and became Adam and Eve. The being "before God created Adam" is the androgynous creature we are discussing here—Adam the androgyne

In the next and last chapter of this book, we will explain why the Cabala said that "this being was man only." It is for the same reason they were called only "the sons of God." But think about it. How could a being that could produce children be "man only?" That is ludicrous. **The significant point is that this singular being that "God created before Adam" could produce children—all by itself—without a sex partner!**

5. Though the "gods" did reserve the right to have occasional sex with a human female or male that really struck their fancy. Hercules and other "heroes" may have actually been the biological offspring of these unions. Originally, all humans were the "sons and daughters of the gods," as the result of the genetic creation of the race of Adam.

6. **Lesbians and homosexuals:** For those who believe the "Lord" was against homosexuality, what they don't realize is that the "Lord" was against ALL forms of sex for humans! *The initial plan was that the race of Adam would not need or desire with anyone or anything other than itself.* That meant that we were genetically engineered to be sexually attracted to ourselves.

Thought: Are homosexuals and lesbians merely

those humans who have a race memory bleed-through, a psychic genetic bleed-through from this initial period when the first humans were androgynous and were genetically engineered to be auto sexual (self -reproducing and sexually attracted to ourselves) or to inadvertently desire the same sex, i.e., the same sex as ourselves? Was part of the reason that the androgynous race of Adam failed was because there was a psychological factor in humans that the Anunnaki had not anticipated? No matter how convenient, no matter how much we were attracted to ourselves, we don't want sex just with ourselves.

We admit that this just an extrapolation. But it would explain why there has always been a third sexuality among humans females, males, and homosexuals. They are those humans who are born with the genetic memory (imprint?) of that time. Perhaps, they are even the human species' subliminal desire to never forget that time.

7. **Plan A.** This first attempt was based on Anunnaki belief that the problem of entrapment could be solved purely with genetics—that purely by physiological means or by creating a homogeneous biological entity that would not need a sexual partner to reproduce. The not physically needing a sex partner to reproduce was the key factor the Anunnaki were banking on to solve the problem of entrapment, or at least the sexual part of it.

In the last chapter of this book, we will examine how it eventually dawned on the Anunnaki that the answer was only partially physiology or genetics. The more complete solution was not just genetics, but also must incorporate psychology , or how to make convince humans NOT TO WANT to have sexual intercourse. This realization was the beginning of Plan B, i.e., using religion, virtue (virginity), and sexual morality as psychological devices of control.

8. **Psycho-sexual equivalent?**: An extrapolation of this theory is that the "gods" sought, with the splitting of humans into male and female sexes, a psycho-sexual equivalent to the race of Adam desiring sex with the mixtures and with the animals. That is, they sought a human species equivalent to the race of Adam desiring sex with the mixtures and with the animals. That is, they sought a human species equivalent to the sexual variety that was obtained with having sex with a unicorn, then perhaps a sphinx or a centaur or a satyr. Could the creation of humans in ethnic and racial classes have been an attempt by the "gods" at a psychological equivalent to this sexual variety that had become forbidden with the animals and the mixtures?

Chapter 7. End Notes:

1. Adding to this theory is a very curious fact: Sumer was perhaps the very first highly advanced civilization humans have ever known. They were the first to create writing and reading. Theoretically, as the first high culture and language, it should have been a language standard. Many cultures should have a knowledge of

how to speak Sumerian. Yet, no one speaks Sumerian or knows how the cuneiform images are pronounced. Few can even read this first language.

2. The phrase "which were of old" indicates that this account had been written long after the giants were destroyed.

3. **The Prime Directive:** Isn't it interesting that the "gods" very attempt to help or rescue humans creates a sub-race of giants that are both worshipped (a giant step in the wrong direction) and also devoured the people? Their very attempt to help causes them to indirectly destroy the people they are trying to help. Apparently, the Anunnaki missed those episodes on Star Trek about the Prime Directive.

4. *When God Was a Women*, by Merlin Stone, 1976.

Chapter 8. End Notes:

1. **"Goat-demons":** After the Anunnaki genetically engineered the "model" man, Adapa (Adam), the new humans existed right along side the hybrid creatures—two distinct races of human life-essences. According to the Edgar Cayce readings, the new humans (the race of Adam) lived side by side with unicorns, dragons, mermaid, etc. until about 9,000 B.C. Erich Von Daniken also claims to have found texts indicating that some of the hybrid creatures *"spent their existence as temple animals and seemed to have been the spoiled darlings of the populace"* (Gods From Outer Space). Suggesting that ancient humans not only knew of these creatures but had

incorporated them into their societies.

Knowing human nature as we do, it would have been necessary for the new humans to have had a derogatory name by which they referred to the entire race of the mostly mentally inferior hybrid creatures. The "gods" had given the new humans (the race of Adam) "smooth skin" like they had. Since the hybrid creatures all had either shaggy coats, fur, scales, or feathers, the lack of smooth skin was that was chosen to denigrate. The derogatory ancient Hebrew word for the hybrid creatures was "hairy ones. It was a word that also meant "wild ones." It was a racial slur like darkie, redneck, or queer.

However, "hairy ones," or "wild ones" is the *translated* meaning. The word itself is "demon." "Demon" originally meant "wild ones," or "wild ones," it was a racial slur coined to denigrate the mixtures, i.e., Lilith was a demon." Its original use was to describe the pan-like creatures, later to be called "satyrs."

2. According to *The 12ᵗʰ Planet*, "God" (Yahweh/Enki) did NOT order the Flood. The Flood was a naturally occurring catastrophe that the orbiting spacecraft flight crew spotted on their instruments. The *Enuma elish*, the original text, say that the decision of the "gods" WAS NOT TO WARN the humans of the coming catastrophe. The change was made in Genesis probably to make the Anunnaki seem more godlike—more powerful than they actually were.

3. **"Stones of emptiness"???:** Insubstantial substance? A reality that is not there? An illusion? A reality without foundation? A false reality? Hollow?—Our guess is **an existence without foundation.**

4. Does the author continue the "stones of emptiness" metaphor here?, i.e., metaphorically "constructing" [insubstantial] palaces and fortresses out of these "stones of emptiness"?

5. **The "lines of confusion:"** The reference to the mixtures as "the lines of confusion" is implied in the Leviticus 18:23 verse:

> *"Neither shall thou lie with any beast to defile thyself therewith; neither shall any woman stand before a beast to lie down thereto: it is **confusion.**"*

Chapter 9. End Notes:

1. *The Complete Idiot's Guide to Lost Civilizations*, by Donald P. Ryan, Ph.D.- Alpha Books – 1999.

2. *Babylon A History of the Greatest City of the Ancient World and Its Rediscovery by Modern Archaeologists*, by James Wellard – 1972.

3. *Ibid.*

4. *Ibid.*

5. *Ibid.*

6. The Dogon call this star *Digitaria*. After the tiniest seed they know.

7. There was a Zecharia Sitchin web page that claimed that Oannaes was a member of the Anunnaki in a "wet

suit" or some apparatus that would allow this Anunnaki to remain submerged. Thus giving him the appearance of being an amphibian.

The problem with that argument is that Oannes was not the only bizarre creature depicted in Babylonian art. There were many types of "mythological" creatures depicted. Plus, the use of the terms Musarus and Annedotus indicates that the Babylonians were sophisticated enough, i. e., smart enough to know here is no "god" in a wet suit. The "gods" always landed from the skies. That he went to war with one of his uncles either Enki or Enlil, and that he also got into several spats with Ishtar, his cousin. Mostly they were turf wars; who would be the "god" of a particular geographic area in Egypt or Mesopotamia.

Chapter 10. End Notes:

1. **Original Sin:** This tampering with creation by the human life-essences was the "Original Sin." Adam and Eve and the serpent was a fable partially designed to preserve or record this transgression. But it all began with the entrapment. The original sin was creating the dream-body thought-form projections and having sexual intercourse with the animals.

   This period of the early humans was known by several code names: The second root race, daughters of men, pre-Adamite humans, hybrids, mixtures, things, and demons. "Demon" meant "hairy ones" and was a racial slur, since the race of Adam all had the "smooth skin of the gods" and the mixtures—the daughters of men did not.

2. **Abduction theory:** No longer trapped in dream-body thought-form projections, but still trapped in physical forms that may not be the most advantageous to returning to the "homelands' of the higher vibrational realms.

We assume that the creation of Adam and Eve represents a finished product, but what if it doesn't? What if the genetic engineering of Adam and Eve (a hybrid species—part alien and part higher primate—that we are the physical representation of were NOT the finished product, but merely the best the aliens could do at that time: Given that they were working with chimpanzees as the highest earth primates available, even though they were encoding the chimpanzees with their own genetic code, may be the best they could do then was to create Adam and Eve, wait for the evolutionary effects their DNA would have on the new hybrid creatures (us) to fully kick in, then periodically make adjustments, i.e., periodically abduct bunches of humans and infuse them with more of their DNA.

In this light, Adam and Eve were NOT a finished product but only the beginning stage of a work in progress. So that the alien "gods" are STILL creating Adam and Eve, the "safe" vessel to incarnate into.

3. Newsweek feature article "Science Finds God," by

Sharon Begley (July 20, 1998).

4. *Ibid.*

5. *Ibid.*

The Genesis Conspiracy. End Notes:

1. The idea of "helpmate" has multiple meanings, as we will explain shortly. "Helpmate" also smacks of the alien "accent," that is, words with double or triple meanings.

2. By being subservient and becoming "property" of fathers, brothers, and husbands, women "helped" men curtail their sexual nature, i.e., "helpmate."